The Octogenarian Handbook

Delaying the 5 Ways of Dying

(and there are only 5 ways to die)

PETER SAXTON SCHROEDER

Copyright © 2024 Peter Saxton Schroeder

All rights reserved. In accordance with U.S. Copyright Act of 1976, the scanning, uploading, and electronic sharing of any part of this book without permission of the publisher constitute unlawful piracy and theft of the author's intellectual property. No part of this book may be reproduced in any form by any electronic or mechanical means (including photocopying, recording or information storage and retrieval) without permission in writing from the author or publisher. Thank you for your support of the author's rights.

Published by Richter Publishing LLC
www.richterpublishing.com

Book Cover Design: Jessie Alarcon

Editors: Austin Hatch, Abigail Bunner & Elizabeth Pottinger

Additional Contributors: Tara Richter

Book Formatting: Austin Hatch

Inside Artwork Created by Microsoft Designer AI

ISBN-13: 978-1-954094-59-8

DISCLAIMER

This book is designed to provide information on Octogenarians only. This information is provided and sold with the knowledge that the publisher and author do not offer any legal or medical advice. In the case of a need for any such expertise consult with the appropriate professional. This book does not contain all information available on the subject. This book has not been created to be specific to any individual people or organization's situation or needs. Reasonable efforts have been made to make this book as accurate as possible. However, there may be typographical and or content errors. Therefore, this book should serve only as a general guide. This book contains information that might be dated or erroneous and is intended only to educate and entertain. The author and publisher shall have no liability or responsibility to any person or entity regarding any loss or damage incurred, or alleged to have incurred, directly or indirectly, by the information contained in this book or as a result of anyone acting or failing to act upon the information in this book. You hereby agree never to sue and to hold the author and publisher harmless from any and all claims arising out of the information contained in this book. You hereby agree to be bound by this disclaimer, covenant not to sue and release. You may return this book within the guarantee time period for a full refund. In the interest of full disclosure, this book contains affiliate links that might pay the author or publisher a commission upon any purchase from the company. While the author and publisher take no responsibility for any virus or technical issues that could be caused by such links, the business practices of these companies and or the performance of any product or service, the author or publisher has used the product or service and makes a recommendation in good faith based on that experience. All characters appearing in this work are fictitious. Any resemblance to real persons, living or dead, is purely coincidental. The opinions and stories in this book are the views of the author and not that of the publisher.

DEDICATION

This book honors all those born in the 1940s and therefore are attaining Octogenarian status in this decade.

Never before have people in any population decade lived longer and healthier lives.

Sending good wishes in hopes that all you 80-plussers—and those that follow—will continue to thrive as a result of better health care, higher standard of living, and—in small part—from suggestions in this book.

Peter Saxon Schroeder

Table of Contents

PREFACE ii
INTRODUCTION vii
1 CONTROL BUNKER 1
2 DEATH BECOMES REAL 7
3 ACCIDENTS 25
4 AILMENTS 51
5 ATTACKS 85
6 ARRANGED 103
7 AGING 127
8 A FINAL WORD 155
EPILOGUE 161
ABOUT THE AUTHOR 165

$(+8) + (+2) = (+10) = -(-10)$
$(+8) - (+2) = (+6)$
$(-8) - (-2) = (-6)$
$(-8) + (-2) = (-10)$

$(+35) \times (+1/7) = (+5) = -(-5)$
$(+35) \times (-1/7) = (-5)$
$(+35) \times (-1/7) = (+5)$
$(-35) \times (-1/7) = (+5)$

$+ \quad - \quad \times \quad / \quad =$

$(+10) \times (+10) = (+100)$
$(-10) \times (-10) = (+100)$
$(-10) \times (+10) = (-100)$

$(+2) - (-8) = (+10)$
$(-2) + (-8) = (-10)$
$(+2) + (+8) = (+10)$
$(+2) - (+8) = (-6)$

PREFACE

Remember the math concept we all learned in fifth grade but could never really understand? If two negative numbers are combined in a certain way, the result is a positive number. That implies two *"no's"* mean *"yes."* When you think about it, the sentence, "I am not unhappy with his decision," actually means "I am happy with his decision."

We understand the concept of a positive number, but it's difficult to comprehend what a negative number represents. We can grasp the meaning of, say, five apples, but what does it mean to have negative five apples? Is it the same as saying we don't have five apples?

But let's go on from here. Combining five apples and three apples gives us eight apples, which is logical. But math teaches that if we have negative five apples added to negative three apples, the result is negative or minus eight apples. But if we have negative five apples and subtract negative three apples, we have negative two apples. More confusing, if we have negative five apples and subtract negative eight apples, miraculously we end up with three real apples that somehow appear out of nowhere. Don't try to figure it out; that's just the way it is.

Now let's go a step further and consider multiplication and division with negative numbers. Two negative numbers if multiplied or divided yield a positive number, which makes no sense in practical terms. If negative 10 apples are divided among negative two people, that means mathematically each negative person gets five apples. But a negative number multiplied or divided by a positive number is always negative. Likewise, a positive number divided or multiplied by a negative number is also negative. If two people divide 10 negative apples, they each get negative five apples.

But what does this mean in real life. We say that two wrongs don't make a right, but let's reconsider that. If I say I don't like not exercising every day, I'm implying I do like daily exercise. So instead of explaining how to exercise every day, I can explain to someone various reasons not to exercise daily. Then, knowing these reasons, the person can take steps to avoid them.

A couple of other examples: If I say he doesn't like not eating apples (two negatives), it literally means he likes eating apples. "She doesn't want not to be happy" (or, more commonly, she doesn't want to be unhappy – since *"un"* is a negative) means she wants to be happy. "He doesn't want not to live to age 80" means he wants to live to 80. So in the real world, two negative concepts can often imply something positive.

I will use this double-negative-equals-positive approach in discussing the five ways to live as an Octogenarian. Rather than enumerate the positive things to do to lead a happy, healthy life, I'll examine the things not to do to not lead an unhappy, unhealthy life. (But watch out! That sentence uses a Triple Negative because *"un"* is also a negative!)

The extreme of living an unhappy, unhealthy life imperils one and can lead to death, the extreme of a negative outcome.

So, let's turn the approach around with the two negatives and discuss the things not to do that will lead to not living, which is, in other words, death. Once we understand this approach, we simply have to do the opposite, namely not do the things that lead to death. Herein lies my approach to the ways to live as an Octogenarian. The goal is to minimize the chances of dying from each of the five ways of dying.

And there are only five ways you can die, as explained in the following chapters.

IF YOU'RE CONFUSED, RE-READ THIS PREFACE UNTIL YOU GRASP THIS APPROACH OF A POSITIVE DERIVED FROM TWO NEGATIVES. THEN CONTINUE READING TO LEARN WHAT NOT TO DO IN ORDER NOT TO DIE TOO SOON.

Peter Saxon Schroeder

NONAGENARIAN

CENTENARIAN

OCTOGENARIAN

SEXAGENARIAN

SEPTUAGENARIAN

INTRODUCTION

Congratulations to those who have reached your ninth decade and attained the status of Octogenarian. Having endured through all the childhood diseases, the risks inherent in daily life, the stress of the work years, and the ever-pervasive threats in our world today, you are indeed survivors. Chances are that you have had your share of these many setbacks, but thanks to our modern medical system and your own personal resilience, you are still alive.

The result is that you have reached this point in life stronger and more determined than ever to enjoy life to its fullest. Unfortunately, according to statistics, over the course of these eight decades you have lost about 25 percent of your childhood friends, college classmates, and work colleagues. Having all-too-often felt the pain of these losses, you are more likely than ever to recognize the dearness of each day—each moment—of life.

I have written this book ostensibly for Octogenarians (a word I have capitalized throughout the book since they are my primary audience), because

I also am one. Likewise, all my childhood friends, those who are still with us, are now Octogenarians, as are my former work colleagues and classmates from high school and universities.

However, this book is equally applicable to Sexagenarians and Septuagenarians who are coming into their later years as well as to Nonagenarians and Centenarians who have already been here for a while. In fact, this book is for all those who hope one day to become Octogenarians, which includes just about everyone on the planet, when they consider the alternative.

The approach I propose is simple. My focus is how to maintain mental and physical health by avoiding imperiling ourselves in a way that leads to disability or death. What makes this approach so simple is the recognition that there are only five pathways to death—yes, only five. Once we understand there are only five ways to die—no other options exist—we must learn the steps to take to minimize our chances of traveling along each of these pathways.

Of course, while there are no assurances that the steps we take, will guarantee that we stay off these five deadly pathways, our efforts will nevertheless lessen the likelihood of finding ourselves moving in any one of these dead-end directions. But here's the tough part: Assuming we have a choice of how to die (of course, we typically don't), which of these five would we choose? No other possibilities exist, so although we can try to avoid them all, one of them has our name on it.

Be that as it may, the choice is not so macabre as it may seem. For most people, if we don't find ourselves on one of the other four pathways, there is one optimum way to pass from this world. Having said that, certain circumstances may lead some of us to prefer one of these other four instead.

In order to avoid a negative overtone to this book, the following chapters don't talk about how to die. They take a more positive approach by explaining the five ways not to imperil yourself. Each chapter outlines ways to lead the safest, healthiest, most meaningful life possible.

The problem with enumerating the ways to live a happy, healthy life as an Octogenarian, or at any age for that matter, is that the list is endless. There are as many things one should do as things one should not do. Enumerating the *do's* and *don'ts* could go on forever. Consequently, such enumerations are not of much help.

Furthermore, although we already know them all, there are so many *do's* and *don'ts* that we can't remember each of them. Even if we could keep all of them in mind all the time, our minds would be crammed so full we wouldn't be able to think about anything else. In fact, we would probably go mad.

The list of *do's* includes such things as: wear your seat belt, get regular physical exams, drink plenty of water, schedule your annual flu shots, get plenty of sleep, eat a healthy diet, exercise regularly, obey traffic laws, keep properly clothed in hot or cold weather, pay attention to your hygiene, maintain an active lifestyle, stimulate your mind, pay your bills, safeguard yourself and your family…and countless more.

Balancing the *do's* are the *don'ts*: don't drink and drive, don't eat too much red meat, don't smoke, don't consume too many carbohydrates, don't endanger yourself, don't get caught up in stressful situations, don't violate the law, and this list goes on forever as well…

With so many things to do, and an equal number of things to avoid doing, we have no simple way to categorize the approaches to take in life to ensure we are always engaged in activities conducive to a safe, healthy lifestyle. As Octogenarians, we have to be particularly aware of our daily dealings, because with the usual deterioration of our minds and bodies inherent in the aging process, we don't have the resiliency to bounce back from mishaps as easily as we did in our 40s and 50s.

The situation is simplified if we return to the double-negative approach, i.e., not, "What should we *do* to live a healthy life?" but rather "What should we *not do* to *not* risk things that would be detrimental to ourselves, the kinds of things that could lead to death?" So now I want to turn to a subject that has, for far too long, been taboo in our culture, namely "death."

But how, you may wonder, do I know about these matters? What qualifications do I have to enable me to delve into this subject of death with any particular understanding? When you're vulnerable, you have the most creative insights and the most inspiring possibilities, which is where my story begins—with my own vulnerabilities.

THROUGHOUT THE WHOLE OF LIFE ONE MUST CONTINUE TO LEARN TO LIVE, AND, WHAT WILL AMAZE YOU EVEN MORE, THROUGHOUT LIFE ONE MUST LEARN TO DIE.

- SENECA

The Octogenarian Handbook

Peter Saxon Schroeder

CHAPTER 1
CONTROL BUNKER

Clustered inside a bunker at the Control Point at Yucca Flat on the Nevada Test Site in a remote section of the central Nevada desert, a select group of men waited nervously as the final countdown began. As a young engineering physicist, I was in awe of those around me—a number of world-renowned nuclear scientists including several Nobel Laureates whose names would be familiar to readers of any books on nuclear and particle physics. Representing two of the three nuclear weapons laboratories, Los Alamos Scientific Laboratory in New Mexico and Lawrence Radiation Lab in Livermore, California, they had traveled to this site to witness an underground nuclear detonation.

I was included in this august group as the representative of America's third nuclear weapons lab,

Sandia National Laboratory in Albuquerque. Also present were high-ranking officials from the Atomic Energy Commission in D.C., along with military officers from the Department of Defense at the Pentagon. As the low man in the hierarchy, both in age and professional background, I respectfully kept my distance from those engaged in hushed conversations. All the while, we all kept glancing at the clocks monitoring the countdown.

With one minute to go, all conversations ceased. Everyone stood up and spaced themselves at respectful distances from each other. Although not sure what this meant, I likewise stood up and moved back from the others. Then we all put on sound-dampening headsets. Moments later lights started blinking from the array of counters, timers, oscilloscopes, and monitors that had remote connections to the instrumentation trailers 20 miles away. Positioned in a perimeter array several hundred yards from the surface of the underground detonation site, these trailers were safely outside the limits of the predicted crater. Instrumentation equipment inside the trailers connected to cables strung out across the desert floor of Yucca Flat to the junction boxes at the top of a 48-inch diameter line-of-sight steel pipe that extended a mile below the Earth's surface. At the bottom of the columnated pipe, a chamber housed the nuclear device, which is essentially an atomic bomb prior to being configured into a weapons delivery system. The purpose of the test was to study ground shock and to assess the impact of the device's blast effects and output of X-rays, gamma rays, and neutrons on the survivability of military hardware.

At $T = 0$, there was no detectable sound or movement. Then, a few seconds later, the shock wave arrived. The ground suddenly heaved upwards with a jolt. Next, the floor and the earth beneath us began to pulsate up and down in a slow rhythm. For nearly two minutes it seemed as if the earth had turned into ocean waves, causing us all to feel slightly seasick. I now understood that everyone had stood up in order to experience these undulations while keeping their distance from each other as we were knocked slightly off balance. Through the windows we watched avalanches reshape the surrounding mountains as rocks and boulders tumbled to the desert floor, stirring up a sandstorm all around us. In the midst of this turmoil, we were suddenly assaulted by the roar of the detonation as it engulfed our bunker. Despite wearing supposedly sound-proofing ear protectors, the blast temporarily deafened me.

At the moment of detonation, the blast vaporized the subterranean rock at the base of the steel pipe, creating an underground chamber filled with superheated radioactive gas. As these gases cooled, a pool of molten rock collected at the bottom of the chamber. Minutes after the blast, as the pressure decreased, the chamber collapsed, causing subsidence and a crater to appear on the surface of the desert. (As the site of more than 1,000 underground nuclear tests that each created a subsidence—not impact—crater, the Nevada Test Site is one of the most cratered landscapes on Earth.) Being well-contained deep in the earth, none of the deadly nuclear radiation vented into the atmosphere, so those of us in the bunker were safe from radiation exposure.

Although I was not exposed at the time of this particular nuclear test, unknown to me, the deadly radiation I had already picked up in my work during the preceding five years had been slowly taking its toll on my bones.

This environment of secret atmospheric and underground nuclear research and testing in remote locations around the world sets the scene for the beginning of my story—the story of why I began at the young age of 24 to be deeply preoccupied with death.

The Octogenarian Handbook

CHAPTER 2
DEATH BECOMES REAL

THE MARSHALLESE STORY

When the U.S. dropped atomic bombs on Hiroshima and Nagasaki in 1945, more than 100,000 people in each city were instantly killed. Outside each of the immediate kill zones, another group approximately the same size received massive amounts of radiation exposure and contracted many types of sarcomas, the most common being Multiple Myeloma, a cancer of the bone marrow. The vast majority died within two years.

This use of atomic weapons in wartime set off the nuclear arms race and America's frenetic rate of atmospheric testing in the Western Pacific. The United States conducted 67 atmospheric nuclear explosive tests in the Marshall Islands between 1946 and 1958. Twenty-three tests were conducted on Bikini Atoll and 44 took place on or near Eniwetok (spelling was officially changed in 1974 to Enewetak) Atoll.

Prior to the first test, code-named Shot Able, the 167 people who lived on Bikini Atoll were forced to move to the neighboring islands of Kwajalein and Ebeye. After Shot Able, scientists determined that soldiers on ships up to a mile away from any similar explosion would be instantly killed.

Operation Greenhouse was a series of nuclear tests conducted at Enewetak Atoll to ascertain the feasibility of thermonuclear weapons and to gain knowledge that would be pivotal in the development of the hydrogen bomb. In November 1952, following the world's first hydrogen bomb test, code-named Shot Mike, the United States conducted its first series of thermonuclear tests, Operation Ivy, at Enewetak Atoll.

On March 1, 1954, the U.S. conducted its largest ever nuclear detonation at Bikini Atoll. Code-named Castle Bravo, the 15-megaton detonation far exceeded the yield expected by scientists. This factor sent radioactive fallout over the inhabited atolls of

Rongelap, Ailinginae, and Utrik. Only after a two-day delay, did the military evacuate more than 300 people from these atolls to Kwajalein for medical care. At 15 megatons, Bravo was not only the largest weapon ever tested by the United States, but it was also the single largest U.S. radiological accident in connection with nuclear testing due to the unanticipated yield and a change in the weather and wind direction.

Rongelap Atoll is just one example of how nuclear fallout and relocation affected the Marshallese, many of whom suffered from deadly burns and radiation diseases. Five hours after the Bravo detonation, a fine, white, powder-like substance began to rain down on Rongelap covering the entire atoll. No one knew it was radioactive fallout, and the children played in it during the two-day delay before the evacuation. In 1957, three years after the detonation and subsequent evacuation, the people of Rongelap were allowed to return home. However, when officials and scientists working for the Atomic Energy Commission concluded that radiation was still a risk due to the effects of Castle Bravo, the inhabitants were re-evacuated.

Residents of the Marshall Islands who received significant exposure to radionuclides due to fallout from testing conducted decades ago continue today to experience an increased risk of developing radiation-related cancers. High levels of leukemia, thyroid cancer, and birth defects are still a major health problem faced by the Marshallese.

The female population of the Islands has a 60 times greater likelihood of cervical cancer mortality and a five times greater likelihood of breast or gastrointestinal mortality than the comparable U.S. mainland population. The male population of the Marshall Islands has a lung cancer mortality four times greater than the overall U.S. rates, and the oral cancer rates are 10 times greater.

In the late 1960s, the Atomic Energy Commission finally declared Bikini Atoll to be safe again for human habitation and started allowing some former residents to return. But this action was cut short a decade later when the people were removed again in 1978 after eating locally grown foods that were discovered to contain high levels of radiation contamination. A study showed that the levels of Cesium-137 in returnees' bodies had increased by 75 percent.

Why is this background relevant to this book? It's relevant because as part of my own background, it had a huge impact on the course of my life and consequently serves as a major stimulus for writing this book.

MY STORY

Jumping forward more than a decade, this fraught-with-hidden-danger world is the one into which I was about to enter after graduating from Princeton University with a Bachelor of Science Degree in Engineering/Physics. At that time, I knew nothing about all this nuclear testing. In fact, no one knew what had taken place in the Marshall Islands during these years because it was all classified information stored in vaults in top-secret military locations.

Sandia National Laboratories in Albuquerque, New Mexico, recruited me to continue my studies in engineering and physics for applications that were not explained at the time. I was told only that Sandia's mission was to design, develop, and test nuclear weapons. Although I didn't know what kind of work I would do, Sandia enticed me with not just an attractive salary, but the offer to pay all my expenses for two years as a full-time graduate student to earn a Master of Science Degree in Electrical/Nuclear Engineering at the University of New Mexico.

Having received several grants from the Atomic Energy Commission (AEC) to develop its Physics Department, UNM had built up one of the top physics laboratories in the country and had attracted an outstanding faculty of acclaimed professors in the fields of quantum physics, materials science, particle physics, and nuclear engineering. Some of these professors would commute down from the Los Alamos Lab where the nuclear fission bomb was developed under the leadership of Dr. Robert Oppenheimer to lecture to those of us who were expected to be the next generation to carry on their research. Such an offer of a generous salary combined with a rarefied study opportunity would have been hard for me to refuse. Even without knowing where it would eventually lead, and certainly not foreseeing how drastically it would affect the course of my entire life, I accepted Sandia's offer. That single decision has made all the difference in the subsequent course of my life.

Upon receiving my graduate degree, I was assigned to Sandia's Field Test Division for three years in Hawaii. My job there was to maintain Sandia's role in supporting a readiness program to resume nuclear testing in the Western Pacific Atmospheric Nuclear Testing Grounds. Site-inspection tours I made throughout these years included visits to virtually every nuclear test location, past and future – Kwajalein, Enewetak, Bikini, Rongelap, Alinginae, Utrik, Baker, and Howland – as well as to the capital of the Marshall Islands, Majuro. I also visited other Pacific sites where detonations had been conducted, namely at Kiribati and Johnston Atoll, from which in 1962 five warheads were shot into higher altitudes and the nuclear tests were conducted in outer space.

Some of my visits were quick in-and-outs because the radiation levels in the soil made the islands still uninhabitable. In visiting these various islands and atolls, I was unknowingly exposed to residual radiation from tests, some of which had been conducted less than 10 years earlier. Although I would have been naïve to think I had not picked up at least some trace amounts of nuclear radiation during these site inspections, I tried to shut thoughts of this out of my mind. In addition to visiting these test sites firsthand, I was given access to data, reports, and photographs documenting the detonation effects on the land, the vegetation, animals, and local inhabitants. In this way I began to learn of the devastating effects these tests had on the local populations that were routinely evacuated to neighboring islands, only to be re-evacuated multiple times in the following years.

Fortunately, both Russia and the U.S. respected the terms of the Atmospheric Test Ban Treaty signed in August 1962, and there have been no further atmospheric tests ever since.

I had taken this assignment in the hope of pursuing more research in nuclear physics, but suddenly a very gruesome picture of what could become reality was beginning to loom on the horizon. Throughout all this time, the dangers of nuclear radiation that so often led to a diagnosis of Multiple Myeloma in those who were exposed was constantly on my mind.

Breathing a sigh of relief when I was transferred, I felt excited about my promotion to manager of the Sandia Lab office at the Nevada Test Site (later named Nevada National Security Test Site), where most of the underground nuclear tests have been carried out. Whereas the atmospheric tests in the Pacific Islands were conducted to determine the yield of the weapons, the underground detonations carried out in Nevada were designed to monitor the effects of the blasts on military hardware.

From 1951 to 1992, the U.S. conducted 1,021 aboveground and underground nuclear detonations at the Nevada Test Site located 65 miles northwest of Las

Vegas. Operation Julin, conducted on the 23rd of September 1992, was the last U.S. nuclear test before negotiations began for the Comprehensive Test Ban Treaty. During my three years at the NTS, tests were conducted on the average of about one a week.

Although the large majority of the Nevada tests were contained below ground, there always was a low level of ambient radiation in the air that my weekly dosimetry badges recorded. Sometimes when those radiation levels were above the acceptable maximums, I had to follow the standard protocol by leaving the site for up to 10 days before returning. Presumably, during my absence the radiation in my body would somehow "dissipate."

More serious were the few underground tests that resulted in "ventings." These would occur between half-a-minute to several minutes following the underground detonation when, at a distance of several hundred yards from ground zero, a plume of black smoke would shoot hundreds of feet into the air and last several minutes. These plumes would occur when the high pressures created by a detonation a mile beneath the Earth's surface would escape through nearby geologic fissures and release into the atmosphere. This highly radioactive effluent would then spread across the desert outside the bounds of the test site toward any communities that lay in the downwind path. More significant for me, on some occasions when these ventings occurred, I was in the path of exposure.

An even more serious risk of my exposure to radiation, however, resulted from my living situation. Oblivious to the low radiation levels that were ever-present throughout the site, I lived in the housing facilities on the NTS site for two years. (The third year I was married and commuted to the site from our home in Las Vegas.) Because we workers at the site were required to turn in our dosimetry badges at the end of each workday, there was never any record of whatever exposure I picked up during off-work hours. At the time, being young and adventurous, I thought nothing of working in a contaminated radiation environment.

THE CONNECTION

The effects of radiation exposure a person receives depend upon three factors: the levels, the frequency, and the duration of exposures. In the case of the immediate survivors of Hiroshima and Nagasaki, the dosage was immense over a short period, so the effects were immediate, and most of those who initially survived died within the following few years. In my case, the low levels of exposure occurred with limited frequency over an extended period of six years, so the effects were not immediate.

It wasn't until a decade passed—after I had earned an MBA Degree from Stanford University's Graduate School of Business and changed careers working as a businessman in Hamburg, Germany—that severe pains started in my back. I knew immediately, based upon my previous study of the effects of nuclear detonations on the exposed populace of the Marshall Islands, that the effects of my own years of radiation exposure had finally caught up with me. Within a month, I was unable to walk. Wanting to get back to the U.S. for medical treatment, I was transported on a stretcher by commercial aircraft to my family home in Louisville, Kentucky. Emergency surgery there succeeded in rebuilding several deteriorated vertebrae, but afterwards came the stunning diagnosis: Multiple Myeloma. "We can treat the disease, but there is no cure," pronounced my dour-faced surgeon when he entered my hospital room the day after the surgery. "It's one of the four terminal cancers. Prognosis, two years, maybe less."

THE CONSEQUENCE

Thus began the most incredible journey of my life, both inwardly and outwardly. The first step was to research the medical literature, but every article I found confirmed the same terminal prognosis. However, Western medicine doesn't have all the answers. Allopathic (conventional) cancer treatment is based upon surgery, radiation, and chemotherapy—so-called "cut, burn, and poison"—which may add only a few months to life while taking an excruciatingly painful toll. No thanks.

Fortunately, there are other medical systems in the world that I could, and did, investigate. First, I consulted with psychic healers from the Philippines who claimed miracle cures, but I found no real help there. Other travels took me to South America. The laetrile clinics in Mexico strung along the U.S. border offered some hope. Chinese medicine suggested another option. But after running into numerous dead ends, I was given several books written by Osho (then known as Bhagwan Shree Rajneesh) about death. His words helped me see death in a new light, not as something to fight to avoid, but rather just as an experience to surrender when it inevitably comes.

With a two-year prognosis and no sense of direction

because other options offered no real hope, I decided to move with my family (a different wife now) and four children, to Osho's ashram in Poona, India. At age 40, I had led a wonderful life, and maybe it was time to embrace death. I had earned enough money to provide for my wife and children once I was gone, enjoyed successful careers, traveled the world, and delighted in many special adventures. Yes, why not just let go and allow death to come as it would? I decided what better place to die than near this remarkable man in India. After quickly disposing of our worldly possessions, my family and I were on our way to India.

Upon our arrival in June 1980, Osho, speaking of a member of his ashram who had died the day before, said, "He was in immense pain, but he remained a witness. He died a beautiful death. That's the way one should die. I teach you not only to celebrate life but death, too, because death is the climax of life, the crescendo. If you have lived your life really, you will celebrate your death, too."

Then along came another twist in my journey. On the advice of friends, I visited an Ayurvedic healer, Balaji Tambe, in his small hut on the outskirts of Poona. On my initial visit, without my saying a word, he gestured for me not to speak and said, "I see what your doctors call cancer and you have come here to die. You are very fortunate because there are only three ways to think about death: accept it, reject it, or ignore it. Everyone ignores it, but you can't. I can help you accept it."

Thus began three years of our regular meetings when he introduced me to different meditations and prepared various Ayurvedic medications and decoctions. Sometimes he put me in an enclosed room where I sat while "treated" by light and sound therapy. Other times in the enclosure he asked me to dance to the meditation music of a sitar and tabla. In addition, he sent me to the burning ghats to watch the bodies burn. He said I should be especially aware of the moment when fluids in the skull heated up and shattered the frontal bones, noting this is the moment the soul leaves the body.

My life now became a strange, but beautiful rhythm as I danced between life in the ashram with Osho and sessions about dying with Balaji. Then a strange thing began to happen. I began to be aware that I was feeling more energy and healing in my body. I dared not hope my Western doctors were wrong in their prognosis, but hovering in the back of my mind was this possibility.

With my constant focus on death throughout these years, I now began to think about the different ways to die. If I don't die from Multiple Myeloma, what are the other ways? I concluded there are only five ways—not more, not fewer—to die. And if we're thoughtful about it, we can do things that might direct us to our preferred way of passing on. Conveniently and memorably, they all begin with the same letter, "A," as will be made evident in the following chapters.

As I write this book, I am now in my middle years as an Octogenarian. During these many decades, thoughts about death have been constantly with me. I have bounced between annual medical checkups in the West and periodic visits to Ayurvedic mystic healers in India. Their messages remain unchanged. My Western medical doctors assure me that Multiple Myeloma can be treated but cannot be cured, even to this day. They admit I have been extremely fortunate over the years. But even after acknowledging that at 40-plus years since my diagnosis, I'm the longest known survivor of this disease, they continue to assert: "Multiple Myeloma is still considered terminal." In the East, the message is likewise unchanged: "Prepare for a beautiful death."

Thus, having been aware of the prospect of dying and constantly watching over the years for the first signs that the dying process has begun, I consider myself a student of death. With my "credentials" in place, I will set forth my analysis of the five ways of dying along with my insights and advice.

Resources Consulted:

("The Marshall Islands and the Bomb," 2024, University of Hawaii Press); ("The Nuclear Catastrophe in the Marshall Islands," Johnson, Giff, 2024); ("Introduction to Marshallese Culture," Alik, T. et al., 2008, Majuro Historic Preservation Office); ("Stories from the Marshall Islands," Tobin, J.A., 2001, Univ of Hawaii Press)

CHAPTER 3
ACCIDENTS

In no particular order, the first on the list of five ways of imperiling yourself or dying is not a health or medical issue. Many people think the top cause of death in the U.S. is heart disease, cancer, or another medical issue, but it's not.

ACCIDENTS are the top cause of death in America, accounting for approximately 225,000 deaths annually. You've probably heard, "Accidents don't just happen. They are caused." This is more than just a familiar saying; it is indeed a truism. Remember, too, that the types of risks change with age. People may guess that the main causes of accidental deaths are traffic accidents or falls, but again, wrong. Traffic accidents and falls rank #2 and #3 respectively among deaths caused by accidents. No other causes of accidental death – including suffocation, drowning, burning, choking, or natural disasters – account for more than five percent of the total. So what's the #1 leading cause of accidental deaths in the U.S.?

POISONING

Yes, Poisoning! With an estimated 102,200 deaths in 2021, accounting for 45 percent of all accidental deaths in the U.S., poisoning ranked as the #1 cause of preventable accidental deaths for all ages combined, according to the Centers for Disease and Prevention.

Most people think of poisoning as a childhood issue, which is true for exposure to poisoning, but not for fatalities. When young children come across medicine-cabinet pills, cosmetics, and cleaning products, the first thing they are likely to do is put them in their mouths. Although dangerous, the resulting illnesses seldom prove fatal.

Fatal and nonfatal poisonings occur most commonly among adults, and are largely attributed to the opioid epidemic. Synthetic opioids laced with fentanyl are particularly to blame. On average, opioid overdoses cause 175 deaths each day. Ninety-three percent of nonfatal poisonings occur in adults between the ages of 20 and 60, and 98 percent of fatalities occur in this demographic. However, the rate of death from poisoning for Octogenarians is low, with 5,200 succumbing to poisoning annually in recent years.

Steps to prevent overdose deaths are obvious but are nonetheless worth repeating. As a precautionary first step, save the number for Poison Control (1-800-222-1222) on your phones, paste it on your refrigerator, and keep it handy throughout your home and office. Read medication labels carefully, adhere to the doctor's prescribed dosage, take care not to mix up your medicines because medicine bottles often look very much the same, and discard out-of-date medicines. Furthermore, Octogenarians can take steps to safeguard young children by being careful to keep medicine cabinets locked and cleaning supplies stored in a secure place.

The general public is likely to consider food poisoning to be a major cause of death. Fortunately, this is not the case. Despite the fact that approximately eight million cases of foodborne illnesses occur every year, the mortality from food poisoning is low. Improper preparation, cooking, and storage of food are the real problems. Therefore, it's helpful to know and trust the source of your food, particularly when there are reports of salmonella outbreaks, mad-cow disease, or poultry and pig diseases. Be aware also of the pesticides, herbicides, chemicals, and other sprays applied to vegetables and fruits, and make up your mind regarding GMO crops. If you have concerns, and your budget allows, opt to buy organic whenever you can.

Livestock are often treated with antibiotics, growth hormones, and other stimulating hormones, so best check into the source of your meats. Phage therapy, which was approved by the FDA in 2006, involves spraying meat with viruses that infect bacteria and thus prevent infection. Because there is no mandatory labelling, buyers cannot know if poultry and meats have been exposed to the spray. Perhaps this is another reason to buy your foods at farmers markets where you can get information directly from the grower.

TAKEAWAY FOR OCTOGENARIANS:
Pay careful attention to the labels on your medicines; be aware of the source and handling of the food you eat.

TRAFFIC ACCIDENTS

Taken together, the top three leading causes of preventable injury-related deaths—poisonings, motor vehicles, and falls—account for 85 percent of all preventable mortalities. Motor vehicle crashes, which account for 20 percent of accidental deaths of any kind, are the second most common cause of accidental death, claiming approximately 45,400 lives each year. Unfortunately for Octogenarians, death rates from traffic accidents peak in their mid-80s, then into their 90s, and continue to be a leading cause of death, second only to falls. Octogenarians suffer a disproportionate share of the 2.3 million non-fatal traffic-accident injuries. Due to their increased vulnerability, the elderly are often permanently disabled as a result.

Although we tend to think of traffic accidents as involving multiple vehicles, the fact is that half of all road deaths are single-vehicle crashes among the elderly. The causes in order of frequency are: inebriation, unbuckled seat belts, speeding, distraction (mostly cell phones), and drowsiness. July and August, the vacation months, are the deadliest. Also, most traffic deaths occur on Saturday, with the second-most occurring on Sunday.

So, what does this mean for Octogenarians? Mostly, it means to be especially aware anytime you step into a vehicle. Before putting your car in motion, go through the following check-list, either mentally (if you can remember) or written on a notepad stored in the vehicle: (1) seat position adjusted, (2) seat belt secured, (3) side and interior mirrors adjusted, (4) radio tuned with the correct volume, (5) interior temperature adjusted, (6) front, side, and back windows clear. Before discounting these reminders, it's important to know that in their late 50s, people begin having lapses of memory, "senior moments," and as time goes on, these memory issues increase in frequency.

Once underway, be aware that your vision and reactions are not as sharp as they once were, so carefully observe road signs and speed limits. If your speed seems uncomfortably high, slow down. Although this may irritate those driving behind you, that's their problem, not yours. There are no legal minimum speed limits on city and rural roads. Stay off freeways if you're uncomfortable driving at highway speeds. Your navigation system can be programmed to avoid highways; it can also guide you to avoid traffic congestion, road closures, and slow-downs due to accidents along your route. Just be careful not to allow your navigation system to become a distraction.

In addition to paying attention to your own driving, be aware of potential accidents in your surroundings.

If a dog or a child suddenly darts in front of your car, can you take evasive action? As you drive past parked cars, are you alert that suddenly the driver could step out and you might clip his door? When a traffic light turns green, do you pause a moment before accelerating to ensure that a car in the cross traffic is not running a red light? And if a cyclist is on the road, are you careful to allow plenty of space?

Many chronic health problems can compromise driving skills. Conditions such as cataracts, arthritis, Alzheimer's, sleep apnea, diabetes (if your blood sugar level suddenly dips), and hearing and vision impairment can cause problems for drivers. Age-related stiffness may cause difficulty when looking over your shoulder to change lanes. In addition, more than half of all licensed Octogenarians take six or more drugs, posing a risk when driving. Many medications can make you drowsy or affect your concentration when reading street signs or noticing traffic markings. Your doctor may give you driving restrictions such as avoiding driving at night or driving slowly on narrow, curvy roads.

It's especially wise for older people to purchase one of the late-model vehicles that are designed to be safer than ever. Since the 2008 model year, side airbags, which improve side-impact protection, have been standard on most cars. According to the Insurance Institute for Highway Safety, older drivers are surviving from crashes that might have been deadly 20 years earlier. Other safety features include rearview cameras that help drivers while backing up, smart head lights that swivel when turning, blind-spot warnings, automatic emergency braking systems, collision avoidance systems, voice-activated warning systems, lane-departure advisory systems, and more.

You may notice indications of your own diminished driving abilities. Warning signs include getting lost on familiar roads, experiencing car accidents or near misses, having trouble parking or turning, receiving tickets for driving violations, finding new dents or scratches on your car, running red lights or stop signs, or crossing lanes improperly.

Thirty-seven states and the District of Columbia have special provisions for mature drivers. Some states require vision tests for renewal starting at age 40. Along with vision tests, other requirements might include in-person license renewals, more frequent renewals, and road tests.

Driving programs such as the AARP courses for

Driver Safety and Defensive Driving can be helpful for senior drivers. These courses provide a good review about safe driving and also offer a reduction in auto insurance premiums. There are other courses that offer tips for driving in snow, rain, fog, or other low visibility conditions.

As a reminder, if you're unsure about your driving skills and don't want to drive, you can call Uber, Lyft, GoGoGrandparent, or one of the other ride-sharing sites. Red Cross may provide transportation for doctor's appointments. If it's just a matter of picking up groceries and sundries, you can contact Instacart, DoorDash, or other delivery services that will deliver your goods to your doorstep.

TAKEAWAY FOR OCTOGENARIANS:
If you feel safe driving, continue to do so, but be extra aware. If you don't feel safe driving, you have a wide array of choices for ride-hailing and delivery services available if you can afford it. If not, there are less expensive ride-sharing services that alleviate some of the cost.

FALLS

For Octogenarians, falls are the leading cause of preventable serious and fatal injuries, and they are the fastest growing rate of any demographic succumbing to falls.

Although falls, which are the third major cause of accidental deaths for all Americans after poisoning and traffic accidents, account for 44,700 deaths, equal to 20 percent annually, they occur mostly among seniors. Every year elderly citizens report 36 million falls, and three million of these who fall end up in the Emergency Room.

Beginning at age 70, the death rate from falls surpasses the number of motor-vehicle and poisoning deaths throughout the remaining lifespan. According to the Centers for Disease Control and Prevention, one out of every four Americans aged 65 and older falls each year. Every second an older adult somewhere in the U.S. suffers a fall. Furthermore, not only are seniors more prone to falling, but they are also more susceptible to injury. Among this age group, eight million falls result in injuries such as a broken hip or head trauma. Fall-related injuries can occur in a split-second. One in five falls experienced by the elderly results in a debilitating injury such as broken bones or a traumatic brain injury (TBI). Ninety-five percent of hip fractures are caused by falling, usually by falling sideways. Also, falling once doubles the chance of falling again. Slip, trip, and fall accidents are the third most common personal injury lawsuits after auto accidents and medical malpractice.

Advances in health care that enable older people to stay active for longer periods of time also raise their risk of falling and incurring head injuries. Octogenarians are at high risk for concussions, a minimal form of traumatic brain injury in which the violent shaking may injure neural networks and tear blood vessels in the brain. There are no drugs to treat a concussion, so the best treatment is sleep, hydration, and minimal physical activity.

In addition to brain injuries, falls experienced by seniors may result in fractures, serious injuries, and premature mortality. Several factors contribute to senior falls, and older adults typically have one or more of these risk factors. Many seniors become less active as they get older, which exacerbates the physical effects of aging. Sarcopenia, which can occur in middle-aged people and those with chronic diseases, is generally associated with older adults and is the prime cause of falling for seniors. Defined as a decline in muscle mass, strength, and function, sarcopenia can result in weakness, fatigue, low energy levels, and difficulty standing, walking, and climbing stairs. Poor nutrition and lack of exercise can increase the odds of developing sarcopenia.

Impaired vision is another major causal factor in falls by the elderly. Failure to see hazards such as steps, puddles, thresholds, and uneven surfaces can cause seniors to lose balance and fall. Vision problems can often be solved by simply getting a new pair of glasses, so have your eyes tested annually.

Various medications increase the likelihood of falling. Sedatives, antidepressants, antipsychotics, opioids, cardiovascular drugs, and other prescribed medicines as well as some over-the-counter medications and dietary supplements can cause drowsiness, dizziness, and excessively low blood pressure. Because almost half of all Octogenarians take six or more prescription medications, adverse drug interactions can have powerful side effects and increase the risk of falling as well.

Various diseases such as Parkinson's, Alzheimer's, neuropathy, and arthritis can affect balance, strength, joint integrity, and cognitive perception. Seniors who use walkers, canes, crutches, wheelchairs, mobile scooters, rollators, and other walking support equipment are also at high risk of falling. Not only does poor physical health decrease a person's ability to respond to hazards that can cause falls, but it also limits the ability to recover from accidents.

Approximately 75 percent of falls happen in the home or nearby premises and account for half of all accidental in-home deaths. Easy-to-remedy causes of home accidents include slippery floors, loose rugs, inadequate lighting, steps without handrails, and clutter strewn on the floor.

Some home improvements can make the house safer and more comfortable for older adults. For example, carpets that prevent slipping, bars and rails that provide support, ramps and lifts that improve accessibility, good lighting that enhances visibility, and rugs and runners that are firmly attached to the floor can all reduce the risk of falls and injuries for seniors in their living areas. Similarly, bathrooms can be modified with mats, low-rise tubs, toilet-seat risers, bars, rails, nightlights, and moderate water temperatures to prevent slips and burns. Outside the home, walkways should have railings and level, well-lighted surfaces. Older adults should also avoid using ladders and step stools, as even a small fall can cause serious injuries.

In addition to being caused by failures to perceive

hazards, falls can all-too-often be caused by not having the proper support and tread on your shoes. Experiencing foot problems that cause pain, or wearing unsafe footwear such as backless shoes or high heels, can also increase the risk of falling. Occupational therapists recommend shoes with flexible, non-slip soles that provide heel support and are easy to put on and take off. Eliminating the need to bend over to deal with fasteners or tie shoelaces, no-tie shoes can be easily slipped right on from a sitting or standing position. The use of hook-and-loop straps such as Velcro allows this type of shoe to be fastened from either side. Lightweight rubber soles reduce the weight of shoes, and orthotic inserts absorb shock. Supportive and grippy outsoles provide a steady step, thus reducing chances of slips and falls.

There are two types of balance: static and dynamic. Static balance is remaining stable while standing still. Dynamic balance is remaining stable while moving. Wide-heeled, flat-soled shoes with good traction and firm support for the arch, toes, heel, and ankle are best for maintaining overall balance. Shoes can be custom-fitted to correct for pronated or supinated feet. For those with difficulty bending over, opt for hands-free sneakers or supportive slip-on shoes. Also useful are adaptive devices such as shoehorns, reachers, or dressing sticks.

Just as important as preventing falls is knowing what to do when you realize you're about to fall. Controlling a fall may help make its impact less severe. Sideways falls, the most common, are the number one cause of hip fractures. If you feel you're going down, avoid the common instinct of putting your arm down, which could break your shoulder, elbow, or wrist. Bend your knees, tuck your chin, go limp, and collapse onto your lowermost thigh rather than onto your hip. If you panic and tense up, you'll likely get hurt. In the event of a forward or backward fall, stay as relaxed as possible, tuck your chin to your chest, and try to land on the front of your thigh or your butt to avoid landing on your hip.

In the event you do fall, stay as calm as possible, take several deep breaths, and try to relax. Remain still for a few moments as you recover from the shock of falling and evaluate your condition to determine if you are hurt. If you think you can get up safely, roll onto your side and wait a few moments while your body and blood pressure adjust. Then get onto your hands and knees and crawl to a chair. With hands on the seat, position one foot flat on the floor while your other leg remains in a kneeling position. From this position, push yourself up and turn your body to sit in the chair.

If you are alone, get into a comfortable position and wait for help. In anticipation of a possible fall, keep a mobile phone with you or wear a special necklace or bracelet that can be used to activate a response system. Most smart watches have this capability as well. After a fall, it is a good idea to get checked out. Even if you don't think you're hurt, report the fall to your doctor.

The best way for the elderly to avoid falls is to build muscles, strengthen balance, and stabilize their gait. A sedentary lifestyle does nothing to promote a healthy body, so choose a way to engage in regular exercise by doing yoga, Pilates, or tai chi, which can all improve balance and help to keep muscles strong enough to prevent a fall entirely. You can also practice standing up from chairs without pushing on the armrests, and practice getting up from the floor without using props. Strength training by lifting weights or using resistance bands can reverse loss of muscle mass and correct general weakness as people age. The main thing to remember is whatever you do, keep moving. Failure to engage in even mild exercise on a regular basis results in reduced muscle mass and strength, decreased bone mass, poor balance and coordination, and reduced flexibility. Not only does overall deconditioning increase a senior's risk of falling, but it also increases the likelihood of incurring a serious injury and facing a longer, more difficult recovery from a fall.

There's good news and bad news for the elderly in general, and for Octogenarians in particular. The bad news is total accidental fatalities in the U.S. claim the lives of, as mentioned, 225,000 people annually with the breakdown by cause as follows: 102,200 poisoning fatalities; 45,400 traffic fatalities; 44,700 fall fatalities. An additional 32,600 preventable fatalities, representing 15 percent of accidental deaths, are due to choking on inhaled or ingested foods; fire and smoke; drowning; suffocation; insect bites and stings; bicycle crashes; train, plane, and other transport crashes; storms and natural disasters; electrocutions; extreme temperatures; lightning strikes; sharp objects; dog attacks; unintentional gun discharges; and other accidental causes—rates that are quite low for all ages.

The good news is that most accidents prevalent among the general population are not significant for the elderly. After age 60, deaths by poisonings and, because many elderly no longer drive, traffic crashes rapidly decline. However, the risk remains high for seniors who continue to drive themselves.

There is only one great hazard due to accidents, namely falls, which rapidly increases beginning at age 60. Falls become the major cause of death in the country for those after age 70 and reach their peak for Octogenarians. At age 80, falls account for more than 80 percent of the country's accidental deaths, and in the late 80s the rate rises to 95 percent.

TAKEAWAY FOR OCTOGENARIANS:
The best prevention steps to avoid falls are maintenance of good vision, hearing, and physical strength; removal of environmental hazards; observance of uneven surfaces; use of handrails on steps and in bathrooms; wearing sturdy shoes with good treads; and using assisted walking devices as needed. In essence, be prepared, be aware, and be careful!

GAIT, POSTURE, & BALANCE

As an Octogenarian, you'll have recognized that your bone density and muscle mass have decreased, your reaction times are slower, and your balance may sometimes be unsteady. Because your body doesn't move as easily and fluidly as it did in your early adult years, you need to make some lifestyle adjustments.

Among other things, you'll notice your gait is slower in crowds at airports or other public places where everyone is passing you. That's because your leg muscles are weaker, and you've lost the knack of propelling yourself quickly with your feet. These days when you walk, you need to make a conscious effort in order to move as well as you previously did without thinking about it.

Here are a few tips to think about as you walk: with every step, rather than just lifting your back foot to swing it forward, push off forcibly from the ball of the foot. Otherwise, your steps will be more of a shuffle than a proper gait. Engage your quad muscles to raise the back foot and, with definite force, kick it forward. As soon as your heel touches the ground in front of you, without a pause be quick to start the push-off with the rear foot. When walking along an airport concourse, for example, follow behind a younger person about your size who has the same stride. Pace yourself so that your steps match that person's cadence and adjust the rhythm of your feet so they raise and lower exactly the same as the feet of the one you're following.

Maintenance of balance is another ability that diminishes with time, so you need to compensate in order to avoid the risk of falling. A fall is imminent if your center of gravity (CG), which is located in the middle of the lower part of your torso, shifts over the outside of either leg. When we're young, we automatically sense when we're likely to fall and quickly self-correct by moving a foot in the outward direction to bring the CG back to somewhere between the legs. But as elders, if we are too slow to respond to a shift in our CG, over we go. It's therefore necessary to develop a strategy to ensure the CG remains safely above the space between, and not outside, the feet.

One technique is to follow the protocol that every athlete engaged in a contact sport is taught: widen your stance. For example, when a football player is tackled, if his feet are close together, the impact will throw him to the ground. But if his feet are planted firmly some distance apart, he is less likely to fall. In the same way, if an elderly person learns to walk with each foot about one shoe-width farther apart than normal—typically with each foot four or five inches extended sideways beyond the usual position—there is less likelihood of falling when walking.

Another way of strengthening one's sense of balance is to practice lifting one leg just slightly for a few moments whenever you're standing around during the day with nothing to do. You can take advantage of the time when waiting in line at the post office or in the check-out queue in a grocery store, or even when talking on the phone. To practice, simply lift one leg about an inch off the ground and steady yourself. If you start to lose balance, just put the foot quickly back down. No one will notice.

Climbing up and down stairs offers another opportunity to work on your balance. First, always be sure to position yourself beside the handrail, keeping it within easy reach. Don't actually touch the railing, however, while stepping up or down. If you hold on, you're likely to become dependent upon the handrail and never learn to compensate for your balance deficiencies.

Another problem with holding onto the railing is that instead of depending upon strength in your legs while ascending, you'll tend to pull yourself up with your arm; likewise, when descending, you'll find yourself braking with your arm muscles. Nevertheless, whatever you do, if you sense you're about to lose balance and fall on the stairs, immediately grab the railing to steady yourself.

Whenever you arise from a sitting or reclining position to walk somewhere, here's another technique to ensure your safe balance. Rising to walk would normally be a two-part movement: get up, then go. However, now it should be a three-part, rather than just a two-part, movement. First, stand up, but don't take a step immediately. Just take a moment to extend your body and legs to your full height and stabilize yourself. Then tip your head to look directly up for a second. This motion will thrust your shoulders back and correctly align your vertebrae.

Taking a short pause before moving is also helpful in case you sense a momentary dizziness, which should quickly pass after you stand up. Some elderly may be on medications that tend to cause light-headedness when rising, so be especially aware if this applies to you. Only after you feel stabilized, balanced, and have inhaled deeply, which takes a second or two, should you begin to walk. In other words, no more "Get Up and Go!" It's more like, "Ready, Get Set, Go," with emphasis on the "Get Set."

There are two reasons an elderly person seldom displays perfect posture when walking. First, with age the vertebrates tend to wear thin as calcium is depleted and the spinal disks dry out. Second, the upper torso muscles tend to weaken, which causes the shoulders to slump. This results in the backbone slumping forward, causing a slightly hunched back known as kyphosis. You may have no symptoms or just mild discomfort, but even a slight hunch will likely create balance issues.

To correct this problem, it's important when you stand up to pause a moment to be certain you've extended yourself into the full upright body position with correct posture. And remember that the trick of looking upwards to see what's directly above your head will help to align your body.

Good posture is important not only while standing, but also when seated. When working at your computer, ensure that the middle of the screen is positioned slightly above the horizontal line of your vision. This will prompt you to sit up straight.

Another technique useful when driving a car is to adjust the inside rearview mirror slightly above your normal eye level. Every time you look in the mirror, this will compel you to sit up tall in order to be able to see what's behind you.

Handheld electronic devices are one of the greatest causes of slumping and poor posture. Most people look downward, often into their lap, to check their cell phone or read their mobile device such as an iPad,

Kindle, smartwatch, digital assistant, handheld computer, or other. Although it might seem awkward, it's better to hold these devices up to your eye level.

TAKEAWAY FOR OCTOGENARIANS:
In matters of gait, posture, and balance, we have to be proactive to ensure that we move safely as we live our daily lives. We can no longer count upon our bodies to automatically respond as they did in our earlier adult years, so pay extra attention to all your movements, and practice adjusting your lifestyle to integrate the various techniques presented above. Continue to engage in regular exercise, eat a well-balanced diet, and take nutritional supplements, especially calcium, as recommended by your doctor.

Resources Consulted:

(Childs, Mel. "21 Home Improvement Ideas on Budget." This Old House, 2024); (Jacobson, Claire. "Reducing falls for older adults: What are the trouble spots in your home?" Scope, 2021); ("Underlying Cause of Death, 2018-2021," 2021, CDC National Vital Statistics System)

Below are contacts for further information about preventing falls:

Centers for Disease Control and Prevention (CDC)
800-232-4636
cdcinfo@cdc.gov
www.cdc.gov

National Resource Center on Supportive Housing and Home Modifications
213-740-1364
homemods@usc.edu
www.homemods.org

Rebuilding Together
800-473-4229
info@rebuildingtogether.org
www.rebuildingtogether.org

National Falls Prevention Resource Center
571-527-3900
www.ncoa.org/center-for-healthy-aging/falls-resource-center/

NIH National Institute on Aging (NIA)
800-222-2225
niaic@nia.nih.gov
www.nia.nih.gov

Stopping Elderly Accidents, Death, and Injuries (STEADI)
800-232-4636
www.cdc.gov/cdc-info/index.html
www.cdc.gov/steadi

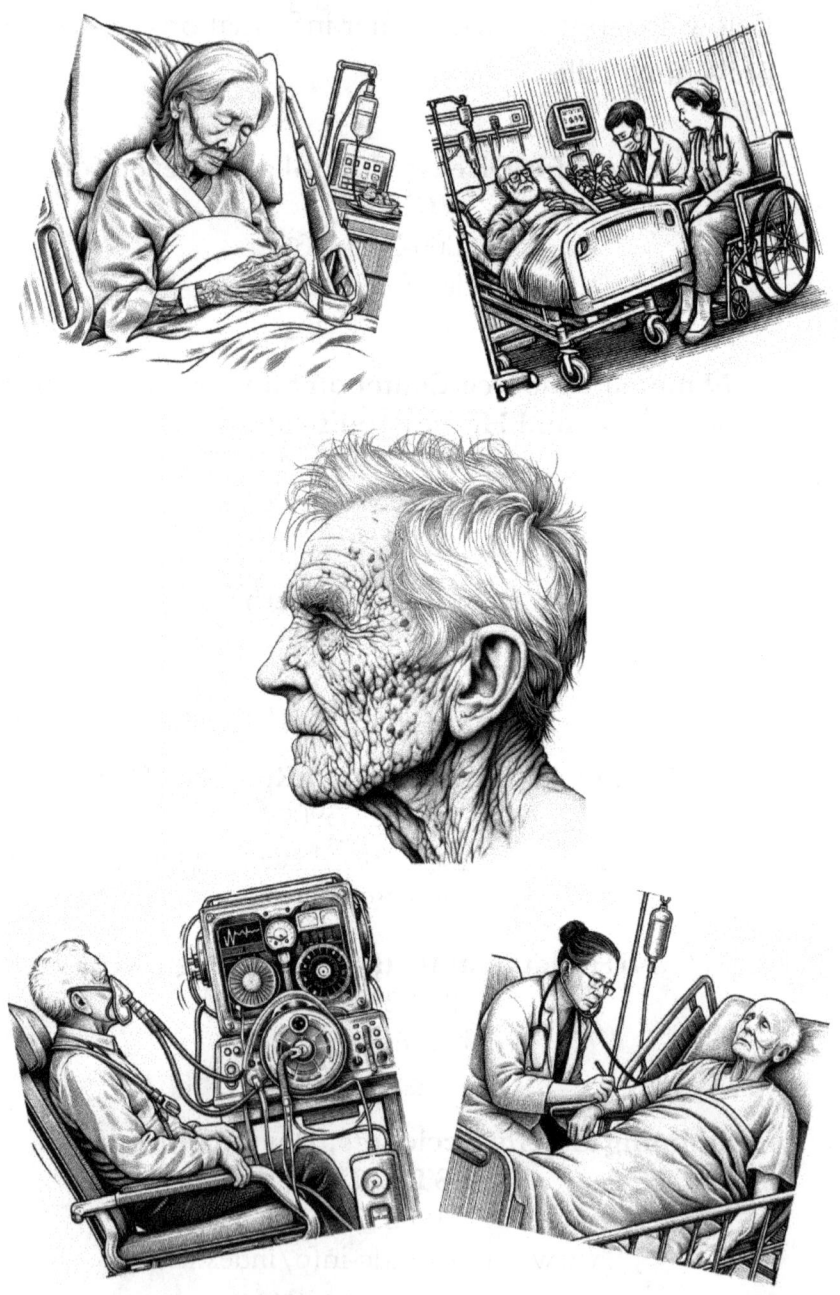

CHAPTER 4
AILMENTS

For those familiar with Abraham Maslow's "Hierarchy of Needs," you, as an Octogenarian, will recognize that at this stage of life it's time to let go of all that drags you down; time to pursue whatever lifestyle makes you feel you are the person you want to be, whether that be an artist, chef, gardener, philanthropist, teacher; time to pursue whatsoever in the world gives you the greatest satisfaction.

But as an Octogenarian, you now face the greatest potential perils to your life, the second of the five "A's" in the list of the five pathways that can lead to deterioration of your quality of life and, in the extreme, to death. So what is this category of threats?

AILMENTS

… or in other words, diseases and illnesses. In the

other four pathways, you can take significant steps to mitigate the chances of experiencing negative impacts. However, apart from adhering to the four commonly known and widely recommended lifestyle behaviors (avoiding smoking, eating healthy, exercising regularly, and watching your weight), there is little you can do to prevent the onset of an ailment.

There are, nevertheless, two major changes Octogenarians must make in their lives, changes that may not be comfortable to carry out, but that are essential. First, however, let's look at the most threatening ailments that Octogenarians are most likely to face.

HEART DISEASE

Claiming 697,000 lives annually, heart disease is the leading cause of death in the U.S. Each year, 2.5 million Americans are expected to have heart attacks, with a disproportionate share of these attacks occurring among the elderly. In 2020, 557,000 fatalities due to heart disease occurred among those 65-plus. This represents 80 percent of the total for that year. Although the heart-disease death rate has fallen for the elderly in recent years, the big growth in the number of America's older citizens resulted in an increase of the total of such deaths. According to a recent heart study, 90 percent of Octogenarians and those who are older have some form of cardiovascular disease.

People aged 65 and older, compared to younger people, are much more likely to suffer a heart attack, to have a stroke, or to develop coronary heart disease and heart failure. Heart disease is also a major cause of disability, limiting the activity and eroding the quality of life for millions of elders. For those older than 75, high blood pressure is the most common heart condition. Coronary artery disease and heart failure are next.

Aging can cause changes in the heart and blood vessels. As you get older, your heart can't beat as fast during physical activity or times of stress as it did when you were younger. However, the number of heart beats per minute at rest does not change significantly with normal aging. A major cause of heart disease is the buildup of fatty deposits in the walls of arteries over many years. High blood pressure and other risk factors, including advancing age, increase the risk of developing atherosclerosis, a condition in which the large arteries harden, stiffen, or become clogged.

High cholesterol levels can also lead to plaque

buildup inside the walls of your arteries. Over time, this plaque hardens and narrows your blood vessels, limiting the flow of oxygen-rich blood to organs throughout your body. Heart attacks, hypertension, diabetes, and heavy alcohol use can all lead to the development of heart disease.

As you get older, it's important to have your blood pressure checked regularly even if you're healthy, because aging-related changes in your arteries can lead to hypertension. You may feel fine but, if not treated, high blood pressure could lead to stroke and problems with your heart, eyes, brain, and kidneys. To manage high blood pressure, exercise, implement dietary changes, and reduce your intake of salt , but medication is frequently necessary. Often you'll need more than one medication to control your blood pressure.

Age-related changes in the body's electrical system can potentially lead to arrhythmias—a rapid, slowed, or irregular heartbeat—and/or the need for a pacemaker. Valves that control blood flow between the chambers of your heart may become thicker and stiffer. Stiffer valves can limit the flow of blood out of the heart, or they may become leaky—either of which can cause fluid to build up in the lungs or elsewhere in the body.

As you age, the heart chambers may increase in size. But despite the increased overall heart size, the amount of blood that a chamber can hold may decrease if the heart wall thickens, and the heart may fill more slowly. Long-standing hypertension is the main cause of increased thickness of the heart wall, which can increase the risk of atrial fibrillation, one of the most common heart rhythm problems in older people.

Other factors, such as thyroid disease or chemotherapy, may also weaken the heart muscle. Things you can't control, like your family history, might increase your risk of heart disease, but leading a heart-healthy lifestyle might help you avoid or delay serious illness.

Nearly half of all heart attacks have no symptoms, and even when symptoms do occur, they may be barely noticeable. That's why regular medical checkups are important. Chest pain is a less common sign of heart disease as it progresses, so be aware of other symptoms including pain, numbness, and tingling in the shoulders, arms, neck, jaw, or back; shortness of breath when active or at rest; chest pain during physical activity; dizziness; and problems doing your normal activities. The aging of other organ systems including the muscles, kidneys, and lungs, can also contribute to heart disease.

With all this going on with our hearts, it's a miracle any of us survive into our ninth decade. But the news about heart disease is not all gloomy, and there are things that we Octogenarians can do to stave off problems. The heart is the easiest organ to monitor by yourself at home. Smart watches can check heart rate as well as give indications of atrial fibrillation, heart flutter, and sinus (normal) rhythm. Various types of home kits measure blood pressure and the level of oxygenation in the blood.

If you have an extra $1,500, you might want to purchase a Home AED (Automated External Defibrillator) unit, but make sure someone in your household or a neighbor who is usually at home is trained how to use it. Although AEDs are scattered in public places such as airports, sports fields, and shopping centers, when a crisis arrives and it's time to use them, people often have no idea what to do. Instructions are given in simple steps; but in a moment of need, it's easy to get confused about what to do. Here is a simple primer.

If someone has fainted and might need an AED, check to see if the person is breathing and has a pulse. If you cannot feel a pulse and the person is not breathing, call for emergency help and prepare the AED by turning it on. It will then give you step-by-step written and voice instructions explaining how to check for breathing and a pulse, and how to position electrode pads on the person's bare chest. Some people may hesitate in using an AED, thinking the victim may simply have fainted and that the shock may have detrimental effects. But don't hesitate to act. There is no need to worry that you might cause some harm, because the machine itself is programmed to determine if the shock is necessary. If it isn't warranted, no shock will be given. When the pads are in place, the AED automatically measures the person's heart rhythm, if there is one, and determines if a shock is needed.

If a shock is indeed warranted, the machine tells the user to stand back and push a button to deliver the shock. The AED is programmed not to deliver a shock if a shock isn't needed. After the shock is delivered, the AED will also guide the user through administration of CPR if needed. The administrator should repeat the process until emergency crews arrive.

Why not consider enrolling in a community education class about how to operate an AED? The American Red Cross, for example, teaches how to use an automated external defibrillator properly and how to perform CPR.

KNOW YOUR NUMBERS

Normal blood pressure should be 120/80. A top number of 121-130 is considered slightly elevated. If the top number exceeds 130 and the lower number is more than 80, that's considered high.

As a general rule of thumb, to find your normal maximum heart rate, subtract your age from 220. A normal resting heart rate for adults ranges from 60 to 100 beats per minute, but the target heart rate for 70-year-olds and older is 75 – 128 bpm according to the American Heart Association. Generally, a lower heart rate at rest implies more efficient heart function and better cardiovascular fitness. Additionally, a total cholesterol level under 200 is considered normal, but the best levels depend upon your age and other heart risks.

Ejection fraction, which is typically measured by an echocardiogram, is the amount of blood ejected from the left ventricle with each heartbeat. A normal ejection fraction is about 50 to 75 percent, according to the American Heart Association. (Please excuse cardiologists who never learned the difference between fractions and percentages because they call EF a fraction but refer to it as a percentage.)

The good news is there are things you can do to delay, lower, or possibly avoid or reverse your risk for heart disease. Adopting a healthy lifestyle is the best way to prevent heart disease. Become more physically active by doing activities you enjoy—brisk walking, dancing, bowling, bicycling, or gardening, for example. Avoid spending hours every day sitting. Also, your function and mobility decrease as your muscles weaken, so being active is the best way to slow loss of muscle and maintain your aerobic capacity. While many older adults remain independent, your ability to engage in moderate to strenuous activity declines unless you act to preserve it.

Follow a heart-healthy diet. Choose foods that are low in saturated fats, added sugars, and salt. As we get older, we become more sensitive to salt, which can cause an increase in blood pressure and swelling in the legs and feet. Be sure to eat plenty of fruits, vegetables, and foods like those made from whole grains, which are high in fiber. Avoid processed foods as much as possible. You can get more information on healthy eating from the National Institute on Aging. You also can find information on the Dietary Approaches to Stop Hypertension (DASH) eating plan at National Institute of Health.

To improve your physical and emotional well-being, keep a healthy weight. Balance the calories you eat and drink with the calories you burn by being physically active. Limit your intake of alcohol. Learn to relax and explore new ways to cope with problems. Consider activities such as a stress management program, meditation, physical exertion, and talking things out with friends or family.

TAKEAWAY FOR OCTOGENARIANS:
Follow a heart-healthy diet; buy a smart watch that can monitor heart rate and also give indications of atrial fibrillation, heart flutter, and sinus (normal) rhythm; home kits can allow you to measure blood pressure and the level of oxygenation in the blood. Not a bad idea to have an AED in your home.

CANCER
Cancer, the second leading ailment cause of death after heart disease, is diagnosed in 1.9 million people in the United States each year and claims 603,000 lives. The American Association for Cancer Research

reported in 2021 that more than 18 million Americans have a history of cancer, yet, due to advancements in diagnosis and treatment, more people than ever are enjoying longer and more fulfilling lives after receiving a cancer diagnosis.

Lung cancer is the leading cause of cancer death, accounting for 137,000 (23%) of all cancer deaths. Other major causes of death in rank order: cancers of the colon and rectum, 53,000 (9%); pancreas, 50,000 (8%); female breast, 44,000 (7%); prostate, 35,000 (7%); and liver, 31,000 (5%). There are 30 other types of cancer—each of which represents only a small percent of the total—that account for the remainder.

Cancer deaths among those over 65 years are particularly high at 441,000, representing almost 75 percent. This is likely due to the fact that cancer treatment can be more challenging and complicated for older adults since they are more likely to have chronic health conditions such as diabetes or heart disease. Even when elderly people are healthy, their bodies will most likely respond differently to treatment than younger people's bodies. For example, older adults are more likely to have serious side effects from chemotherapy.

Unfortunately, unlike for heart diseases, there are no home test kits to detect the possible onset of cancer, with the exception of a home test for colorectal cancer. That's why regular medical checkups and cancer screenings are essential, particularly for the elderly. By the time symptoms occur, the disease has often progressed to an advanced state. Thus the old adage, "The squeaky wheel gets the grease," is wrong. By the time it "gets the grease" it may be too late to save the wheel. Better to monitor all the wheels ahead of time on a regular basis.

Cancer screening tests are designed to detect cancer early, enabling treatment to begin when it has the highest chance of succeeding. Treatment is most likely to be effective before the cancer has had time to grow and spread around the body. Screenings may also detect precancers that can be removed before they become cancerous. The following cancer screening tests are covered by Medicare and are recommended by the American Cancer Society: colon, lung, breast, prostate, and cervical. There is no single diagnostic test for pancreatic cancer.

The main cancer treatments are surgery, radiation, and chemotherapy (facetiously known as cut, burn, and poison). The risks of these treatments can be higher when you are older because your body does not work as well as it did in your middle adult years. Surgery often requires administration of drugs that can stress the kidneys and liver, or it may require the temporary cessation of blood thinning medications. If you have a lung condition such as emphysema or chronic obstructive pulmonary disease (COPD), you may have problems recovering from anesthesia and the medications you get before and during surgery. Unlike radiation therapy and surgery, chemotherapy generally affects your whole body and can take a long time to administer with treatments spread over weeks or months.

Fortunately, the war on cancer is making progress. In the past 20 years, from 2001 to 2020, cancer death rates went down 27 percent. New cancer vaccines are coming on the market that both prevent and treat cancer, and cancer screening tests are helping people catch cancer at an increasingly earlier stage when treatments are most effective. In addition to scheduling regular health checkups and cancer screenings, the elderly should follow the six inviolate rules to keep their bodies healthy: exercise regularly, watch your weight, eat a healthy diet, don't smoke, avoid stressful situations, and maintain an involved lifestyle with significant social connections.

TAKEAWAY FOR OCTOGENARIANS:
Get annual or semi-annual medical checkups that include cancer screenings.

COVID-19

Enough has been reported about COVID-19 that nothing more can be added here. The annual death toll in recent years from this third most deadly disease is 351,000. More than 80 percent of COVID-19 deaths during the first two years of the pandemic were among people aged 60 and older, with the greatest risk concentrated among Octogenarians.

If the history of fighting viral diseases is any indication, medical science is making progress in bringing COVID-19 and its many variants under control, so the infection rate of this virus will likely decline in the coming years, but probably not until the distant future. Therefore, Covid and its many strains are likely to still be around for quite a while. This means that for older Americans the pandemic will continue to pose significant dangers. Until then, everyone, particularly the elderly, should adhere to the standard protocols of wearing masks when in groups, washing hands thoroughly and regularly, and keeping up to date on vaccines and boosters as they become available.

TAKEAWAY FOR OCTOGENARIANS:
Stay up to date with injections and boosters.

DEMENTIA

The term "dementia" refers to the gradual loss of several cognitive or thinking abilities. Over time, people with dementia lose the ability to remember, to communicate effectively, and to use reasoning skills to function in their daily lives. Dementia is a syndrome, not a disease, and isn't a single disorder. It's a blanket term that includes many progressive brain diseases, the most common being Alzheimer's disease, Parkinson's disease, Lewy body dementia, vascular dementia, and frontotemporal disorders. Dementia symptoms such as memory loss may not directly cause death. But the disorders that cause dementia result in the progressive damage to brain and nerve cells, and can lead to pneumonia, strokes, falls, infections, medication mistakes, and malnutrition that are often fatal.

Approximately 6.7 million Americans aged 65 and older suffer from dementia today, according to the latest statistics from 2022 by the CDC, and 75 percent are Octogenarians. The percentage of people with dementia increases with age: 5% of people between the ages 65 to 74, 13% between the ages 75 to 84, and 33% in ages 85 and over. The statistics from 2022 also show that more than 135,000 deaths are attributed to dementia-related diseases, making such diseases the fourth largest factor contributing to medical-related deaths among the elderly. This estimate may be a significant underestimation, because the National Institute on Aging has said that the number of U.S. deaths linked to dementia may actually be as many as three times higher than is reported on death certificates.

TAKEAWAY FOR OCTOGENARIANS:
When you see early signs of dementia in yourself as well as in elderly family members and loved ones, contact a medical professional.

RETHINKING WHERE YOU GET YOUR HEALTH SERVICES

Over the years, the elderly have regularly seen their trusted doctors and been treated for medical conditions at their local and regional medical centers. Now this all needs to change. Although you probably trust your family general practitioner or internist and the specialists who have taken good care of you for years, it's nevertheless time to move beyond them for several reasons.

First, like you, your doctors have been aging and are

coming to the end of their careers. They may not have been keeping up with the latest medical research or been diligent with their continuing medical education or with reading the current medical journals. The best path forward may not be simply to accept your doctor's recommended successors, even if those physicians are highly qualified with degrees from prestigious medical schools in specialties that meet your needs.

The main reason for parting ways with your current medical providers is due to the changes in your needs as you approach Octogenarian status. When people contract an illness in their middle adult years, their bodies respond differently than they do 35 - 45 years later. Unlike in our later years, at earlier stages of life, our immune systems are generally strong enough to keep us safe from pathogens, bacteria, viruses, and germs that we encounter in our daily lives.

With age, the immune system is likely to diminish in strength, and your body won't be able to function optimally in fighting off the pathogens you come in contact with. Some signs that the immune system may not be fully supported include high stress levels, frequent colds, digestive system problems, slow-to-heal wounds, frequent infections, and chronic tiredness.

Muscle mass deterioration, which is characterized by replacement of muscle mass with fatty tissue, occurs as one ages. Muscle deterioration can be accelerated by a sedentary lifestyle or by past serious chronic diseases of the lungs, heart, gastrointestinal system, or kidneys. Chances are that, as an Octogenarian, you have had some serious bouts with several of these conditions.

Loss of reflexes is another characteristic of aging. Diminished reflex responses result from decreased sensitivity of nerves, nerve damage, or as a consequence of any number of chronic diseases. Decreased reflex responses can, of course, increase the likelihood of a senior having accidents of all kinds.

The bottom line is that the elderly body, for a number of reasons, tends to be frailer and less able to care for itself when an illness occurs than in younger years. So, to answer the question of which age group needs medical services the most, it's the elderly. As we age, we need more elder care options such as access to gerontologists (physicians who specialize in treatment of the elderly), and increased availability of skilled nursing facilities, mental health care facilities, cancer centers with fusion treatments, urgent care sites, and PACE (Program of All-Inclusive Care for the Elderly) programs.

Whereas the elderly over age 60 comprise 22 percent of the U.S. population, their medical expenses represent 52 percent of the nation's total medical expenses, and 25 percent of the total expenses are taken up by seniors in the last two years of their lives.

In regard to medications, sometimes the usual prescription to cure or treat an illness can in itself be detrimental for the elderly, particularly when various doctors of different specialties have prescribed multiple medications. Some medications can interfere or interact with other medications, and because the body of an Octogenarian isn't as robust as it once was, risks and side effects can be amplified. It is important to pay attention to such side effects as dizziness, confusion, balance issues and unsteadiness in walking. Inform yourself of these potential adverse reactions for all your medications so you can be aware if any problems arise. Every detail for every medication can be found on the handouts that accompany each prescription and on the Internet as well. Keep each of your doctors apprised of all your prescription drugs, so they can advise you of any possible adverse drug interactions. Also inform your doctors of any supplements you might be taking, because they, too, might potentially interact with some of your medications.

While from time to time people of all ages may feel ignored and dismissed in medical settings, the sentiment is particularly prevalent among older adults. Health care providers often carry biases that slip through and affect patients. Elder patients can experience ageism in any of three ways. 1) Care providers may infantilize elders and talk down to them. 2) Providers may be dismissive of an elder patient's problems. Or 3) providers or caregivers may trivialize issues among older people as so-called "routine" aspects of aging. Whenever these things occur, you should recognize that ageism has come into play, and confront your provider regarding this bias. Speak up for yourself to assert that you want to be treated as an individual rather than grouped into a category and insist that your medical concerns be treated seriously.

Now is the time for the elderly to adopt an entirely new approach regarding how and where they should get their medical care. Time to let go of your previous health care providers and your medical centers, and move to the highest level of medical care facilities available, of which there are perhaps only a dozen or so in the country. Even if you're feeling satisfied with your previous level of care in your locale, it's essential to seek out one of the world-acclaimed major medical centers, at least to get second opinions and a full baseline physical and mental check-up. Among the best medical centers in the country are Mayo Clinic, UCSF, Sloan Kettering, MD Anderson, Cedars-Sinai, Cleveland Clinic, Johns Hopkins, Mass General, Stanford Medical Center, and several others. They all accept Medicare and most other insurance coverage, and will accept anyone either with a medical referral or self-referral. The intake process is similar and straightforward for all these facilities.

My personal experience in this regard may be relevant for others. Mayo Clinic in Rochester, Minnesota, for example, which is, according to some surveys, the top-ranked medical facility in the country and where I go for my medical treatment, asked me to send in all my medical records prior to my first visit. When I said I would send in reports from my doctors, the intake coordinator said this was not needed, only the x-rays, CT scans, lab reports, and original source information. When I asked why I should not include the doctors' and radiologists' reports, she replied politely, but a bit awkwardly to avoid criticizing my previous care providers, that sometimes their doctors at Mayo see things that others have missed, so they want to see the source images. Sure enough, in my case, they did.

When I requested appointments for a general checkup and second opinions, the intake coordinator instructed me to arrive on a Monday and plan to be there for one week. I was curious why she set up only one appointment with a general practitioner if I was to be there a full week. By mid-morning of the day of my arrival, I was finished with my appointment with the GP, but I was in no way through with my Mayo visit. Before I left the doctor's office, he explained that I needed a complete workup for a base-line study. He handed me a full five-day schedule with appointments to see a urologist, oncologist, orthopedist, cardiologist, dermatologist, and endocrinologist. In addition, he scheduled a series of tests that included a PET scan, chest x-ray, urology VB3 test, EKG, and echocardiogram, as well as CT scans of the prostate, kidney, head, and thyroid along with some unscheduled time for follow-up as needed. By the end of the week, Mayo had completed a thorough analysis of my health—an analysis reviewed with me on my last day by the same GP I had seen on the first day. Never before had I experienced such a thorough work-up—one that revealed several medical issues warranting a return visit in the near future.

Elderly persons may claim they feel fine and have no need for additional medical advice. But beware! Symptoms alone cannot be relied upon to indicate the onset of health problems. In fact, if you wait until symptoms emerge to seek medical help, it is often too late. An ailment could already have progressed to a stage 4 level by the time a patient has any symptoms. Another likely scenario is that when seeing a medical provider to check on a minor health problem, routine blood and urine exams may turn up a much more consequential, but now advanced problem, even before symptoms occur—a problem that could have been caught during a normal annual or semi-annual check-up.

It's important at any age, but particularly for those in advanced years, to take responsibility for their health issues instead of blindly following the advice of the medical provider. You can find any detail of any medical issue by searching the Internet, and you owe it to yourself to learn as much about your medical problems as possible. This will enable you to ask important questions and discuss details of your problem with your doctor intelligently. For example, you might ask such things as why he prescribes a CT scan instead of an MRI or a PET scan, why just an EKG instead of an Echocardiogram as well, why not a sleep apnea test, or what about a biopsy of a suspicious growth?

You can research the risks of medications that are prescribed and ask why this one is preferred instead of another, and why this dosage? Take charge of your medical condition; don't hesitate to ask challenging questions about the diagnosis and treatment. When your treatment is underway and you're told to come back in a year for a follow-up checkup and more diagnostic tests, you don't have to settle for that. Know that because you're in an elderly demographic, other negative implications can arise in a longer span of time. Insist that you come back in six months instead of waiting a whole year.

Check out your genetic ancestry through one of the DNA genetic services to learn if you have a predisposition to certain diseases, and be proactive in seeking out tests for verification. You will learn about people from whom you are biologically descended and how any health issues found in their genetic makeup may affect you. Discover how your DNA may impact the way your body processes certain medications and how personalized DNA insight can help you to better understand your health.

With this background in mind, let's review a few sobering numbers. According to reputable medical sources, in recent years the leading deadly ailments in rank order are: heart disease, 697,000; cancer, 603,000; COVID-19, 351,000; Stroke (cerebrovascular diseases), 161,000; Chronic lower respiratory diseases, 153,000; Alzheimer's disease and dementia, 135,000; diabetes, 103,000; influenza and pneumonia, 54,000; kidney disease, 53,000; and the list goes on. Another scary statistic, according to a study by Johns Hopkins patient safety experts, is that more than 250,000 deaths per year in the U.S. are due to medical errors. The newly calculated figure for medical errors puts this cause of death behind COVID-19 but ahead of strokes.

TAKEAWAY FOR OCTOGENARIANS:

As much as you trust your local doctors and regional medical centers that have taken good care of you through your middle adult years, you have to recognize that any health problems will be accompanied by a geriatric overlay that introduces additional complexity. Turn your health care over to one of the country's nationally acclaimed medical centers such as Mayo Clinic,

UCSF, Sloan Kettering, MD Anderson, Cedars-Sinai, Cleveland Clinic, Johns Hopkins, Mass General, or Stanford Medical Center among others.

SECOND OPINIONS

The most important medical advice for Octogenarians is to transfer your medical records to one of the nation's top medical centers. The second most important advice is to always get second opinions. Doing this is an essential step as you take personal responsibility for your health care. The expense of getting second opinions is covered by medical insurance.

Unfortunately, many elderly hesitate to take this step because they feel it indicates a distrust of, and would be offensive to, their doctor. Doctors speak authoritatively when they make a diagnosis and suggest a course of treatment, so it's natural to believe that what they say is correct. But the field of medical science is always evolving with recent research breakthroughs and new medications becoming available, so it's never clear if your physician is totally up to date. Furthermore, doctors often have different ideas about how to treat particular health problems.

To personalize this matter, I'll go into some of the

issues I have encountered when seeking second opinions, which I frequently do. My primary medical centers are all highly regarded medical facilities: Mayo Clinic in Rochester, Minnesota; Virginia Mason Medical Center in Seattle, Washington; Marin Health Clinic and Hospital in Greenbrae, California; and UCSF Medical Center in San Francisco. I am a patient at each of these facilities and have sought second opinions on the following five occasions, each of which has caused me to change the original prescribed treatment.

SECOND OPINION EXAMPLE #1 – Hearing Loss: When tested for my hearing at one of these facilities, I was told I had only minimum loss in my right ear but 85 percent loss in my left. I was fitted with a usual hearing aid in my right ear and a "crossover" in my left that sent the sounds received on my left across to the right hearing aid. It worked fine except I no longer had "localization," meaning I didn't know from which direction sounds were coming. When riding my bike on my daily six-mile rides, I became fearful because I could hear nearby traffic but couldn't determine from where the sounds were emanating. This was particularly dangerous when I would hear a siren, so I would have to stop my bike and look all around to see what was coming.

A second opinion from an audiologist informed me I had been fitted incorrectly and should have two normal hearing aids, because a crossover is recommended only when one ear is so-called "dead," meaning there is 100 percent hearing loss. Concerned about this conflicting advice from two reputable sources, I sought out two more audiologists who tested my hearing. Both confirmed the second opinion, so I was outfitted with two new aids, one adjusted to each ear, and now, happily, I have a normal sense of localization of sounds.

When I returned to my original hearing aid center, they refused, in spite of three contrary opinions, to admit they were wrong. Nevertheless, now, thanks to the second opinion (and my two hearing aids), I have normal hearing.

SECOND OPINION EXAMPLE #2 – Steroid Hip Injection: When diagnosed with "Snapping Hip Syndrome" after reporting pains in my right hip with every step, I scheduled a procedure to get a steroid injection. I was draped on a surgical table and the doctor, using ultrasound, guided a needle carefully into a particular site in the bursa. I was then told I should not repeat this procedure too often because it can have long-term detrimental consequences for the rest of my body. The pain was relieved for about six months, but when it returned, I scheduled a second procedure, and, although this relieved the pain, the doctor advised me not to have any more of these injections.

Six months later I was, again, in pain every time I took a step, so I sought a second opinion at one of the other medical centers where I was a patient. This doctor, during my office visit, quickly prepared a needle and gave me, on the spot, a steroid injection—no surgical table, no draping, and no ultrasound guidance. When I asked why he didn't use ultrasound, he said there was no need because the bursa is so large it's impossible to miss. He laughed when I asked whether I should call his approach "anatomical topography" or "topographic anatomy." He also informed me, contrary to the previous opinion, that I could come in for future injections every three months if needed. He explained there was no risk of long-term problems because the steroid is fully contained in the bursa and thus would have no effects elsewhere in the body.

Consequently, for several years I returned to him for additional injections when the pains reoccurred. Each treatment, which always brought immediate relief, confirmed the wisdom of getting a second opinion.

SECOND OPINION EXAMPLE #3 – Atrial Fibrillation: When a routine physical exam indicated that my heart, which had previously always been in regular (sinus) rhythm with normal beats per minute, showed I had A-Fib and an unusually high heart rate, my cardiologist prescribed medication to reduce the heart rate. Because I said I had no symptoms, the doctor said the A-Fib was not a problem because he had patients who had been living for years with this irregular rhythm. He never discussed a cardioversion procedure that almost always restores the heart to normal rhythms. He also downplayed the effectiveness of an ablation procedure, another common option, in which electric probes, inserted through the femoral artery into the heart chambers, zap and disable the errant nodes responsible for generating electrical signals that cause irregular heartbeats.

During the following two years, I was constantly breathless whenever I exerted myself during bike rides and workouts. Furthermore, I had difficulty breathing at higher elevations when skiing. Consulting an electrophysiologist, I learned that my heart medication prevented the heart from speeding up when my lungs were demanding more oxygen. The electrophysiologist then convinced me to undergo an ablation, which restored my heart to normal rhythm and solved my problem of breathlessness.

Unfortunately, he had not warned me of the dangers of drinking alcohol. As the owner of a wine grape vineyard and a wine-drinker, I continued to drink a glass of wine every evening. Before long I was back with A-Fib. A third cardiologist performed a cardioversion procedure that brought my heart back to normalcy, and she warned me about drinking any type of alcohol anytime in the future. Solving my heart problem ultimately required not only a second but also a third opinion.

SECOND OPINION EXAMPLE #4 – Multiple Myeloma: During the years since my diagnosis with multiple myeloma, my oncologist had conducted annual bone surveys of my "long bones" which would indicate if the myeloma ever became active again. However, after decades of these tests, a myeloma tumor showed up in my sternum, a bone that my original oncologist had not included in the years of previous bone tests. My new oncologist, who said that it's not unusual for myeloma tumors to show up in the sternum, prescribed three weeks of a new radiation therapy that shrank the tumor until it disappeared. Contradicting my earlier doctor, this oncologist explained that PET scans, not bone surveys, are the best method for detecting new tumors, and ever since I have scheduled these scans on a regular basis. In this instance, a second opinion saved my life and put me on a future course to monitor this disease.

SECOND OPINION EXAMPLE #5 – Prostate Disease: My original urologist put me on medication to reduce my PSA (prostate-specific antigen) number, because the high number indicated a risk for prostate cancer. Once it was reduced to safe levels, he said I should take the medication indefinitely. After a year of maintaining a low PSA, I began to have side effects from the medication. A second urologist explained the medication wasn't necessary long-term and suggested I stop taking it, whereupon the side effects immediately disappeared. He informed me of a new, well-accepted medical procedure in the event that cancer should occur. Once again, the second opinion, which contradicted the advice of my first urologist, saved me from additional years of taking a potentially harmful medication.

TAKEAWAYS FOR OCTOGENARIANS:

To minimize chances of imperiling your health or dying from Ailments, exercise regularly; eat a healthy diet; maintain a reasonable weight; minimize stress; and schedule regular checkups with cancer screenings. Where you get your health guidance is important, so transfer your health records to one of the nation's top dozen nationally acclaimed medical centers. Whatever the cause of any illness, early detection and early initiation of treatment are much more likely to improve the outcome than when detection and treatment occur in advanced stages of the ailment. Remember that by the time symptoms occur, it may be too late for effective treatment. And always seek second, or even third, opinions.

Resources Consulted:

(National Institute on Aging, 2024, "Heart Health," www.nia.nih.gov); (Morley, J.E. & Thomas, D.C., 2007, "Geriatric Nutrition," CRC Press) (Octogenarians Blog, https://theoctogenarians.com, "The Octogenarians");

CHAPTER 5
ATTACKS

Mugged in a dark alley, kicked by a horse, or trapped in the rubble of an earthquake—these are examples of how your body can be attacked by man, creatures, and the destructive forces of Nature. Due to diminished body strength and resiliency, the impact of an attack is far greater for the elderly than it would be on those who are younger and stronger.

Following Ailments and Accidents, the third of the five pathways that can imperil senior citizens and may lead to death, particularly for Octogenarians, is yet another "A," Attacks.

ATTACKS BY HUMANS

Attacks, acts of aggression, or assaults (all A's once again) by our fellow beings can occur in any of 12 ways, all of which are easily avoided. First, let's look at a few statistics. Every year in America, 1.4 million people are treated in hospital emergency rooms for assault. Out of 24,600 homicides, firearms account for 19,400. Other intentional murders are committed by stabbing, beating with blunt instruments, drowning, choking, poisoning, electrocuting, torturing, kidnapping, raping/abusing, road-rage crashes, and encounters during thefts/break-ins. According to recent FBI statistics, the American city with the highest murder rate is St. Louis, followed in descending order by Baltimore, Birmingham, Detroit, and Dayton.

Another sobering statistic, according to the Centers for Disease Control and Prevention, is that 60 percent of the assailants were related to, or knew the victim. For homicides, almost 50 percent of crimes were committed by a spouse or partner, parent, child, relative, or friend, so the advice to Octogenarians is to choose your caregivers carefully. A study estimates that one in 10 elderly adults has been subjected to abuse, neglect, or exploitation. As the number of America's senior citizens rises, the rate of violence against them is rising even faster, according to a report from the CDC.

When an attack occurs, the elderly—particularly

those over 80 years—have limited ability to defend themselves. The main reason is that the attack comes as a surprise, there's no time to prepare to defend oneself. Reflexes tend to deteriorate with age, so Octogenarians may lose a few precious seconds trying to figure out how to respond. Once victims assess the trouble they are in, they may not have the agility to move quickly out of harm's way. In addition to diminished agility, the elderly may also have diminished muscle mass, so they typically don't have the strength to fight back. The perpetrators of an attack on an elder are usually younger, stronger, and have the advantage of knowing exactly what they are doing. They have singled out a particular elderly person, anticipating there wouldn't be much resistance. Furthermore, the perpetrator is likely to be holding a weapon, while victims can defend only with their hands. Little can be done to defend oneself when an attack is underway, so in the interest of saving your life, it's usually best not to resist. Simply surrender to whatever the perpetrator is after.

There are different types of attackers, and they are motivated for different reasons. Muggers or criminals may just want your valuables. Others may be looking for something that, in their opinion, is fun to do by harassing you. Alternatively, they could be mentally unstable or under the influence of drugs or alcohol. Or the attacker may want to get rid of you if you are a witness to a crime they have committed.

Your first response to a threatened attack should be to attempt to run away. If this doesn't work, try to figure out what kind of person or persons you're dealing with and why they are attacking you. Talk to them. Ask what they want and if there is anything you can do to stop the attack. If they say they want your valuables, simply relinquish whatever you have. Fighting to try to save a few dollars, credit cards, a cell phone, and a driver's license is not worth the risk of losing your life. These items can be replaced, but your life and health cannot.

The most dangerous attackers are those who seem mentally unstable or under the influence of a substance because they will be unpredictable in what they do next. If the potential attacker is especially menacing or threatening, talking may prove to be useless. Nevertheless, talking to them in a calm manner while backing away is worth a try. Anything you can do to stall may allow for someone to intervene. If you're in a public place where others may be able to help, yell to get their attention.

Attacks with knives, other sharp instruments, or heavy blunt objects can be very unpredictable and potentially lethal. When wielded by muggers or would-be attackers, these hand weapons can cause more damage than a gun. If you're dealing with such an attack where your life is clearly in danger, you may have to try to defend yourself by grabbing a makeshift weapon and attacking the assailant's throat, groin, or eyes. You might want to consider signing up for self-defense classes so you can be prepared for a random attack.

Whereas not much can be done by an elderly person to resist when an attack is imminent, there are many things one can do to prevent attacks from occurring. First, consider your location. Are you in a high-crime area or a location known for the presence of gang members? Are you someplace where there are very few police officers? When out at night, do you stay in well-lit areas and places with many people around? Do you really have to go out at night, and, if so, can you travel by car, bus, or other transportation instead of walking alone? When walking outdoors, do you have someone to accompany you?

Be mindful of your appearance and behavior when walking outdoors. Avoid wearing glittery jewelry, necklaces, and expensive-looking watches that will be apt to catch the eye of would-be robbers. If there's a possibility of encountering an assailant with a knife or other sharp weapon, wear clothing such as leather that can afford some measure of protection. If there is probable danger, consider wearing a stab-proof vest intended to be worn under clothing. Lightweight and thinner than outerwear vests, concealable vests with covert designs are comfortable to wear.

Furthermore, be careful to keep an eye on your surroundings, and pay attention to anyone who seems to be following you. If you feel fearful in a particular area, carry some type of deterrent device such as pepper spray. If someone is stalking you, slip into the nearest building and remain until you feel safe. If you feel threatened, call 911.

When at home, keep your windows and doors locked, or in some cases double-locked. At night, keep window shades drawn and maintain outdoor security lighting and alarms as well as motion detectors around your property.

Although owning a gun makes some people feel safer, according to statistics having a gun in your home is more dangerous for you and your family than not having one, especially if you have young children or teens. A study in the Annals of Internal Medicine concluded having a firearm in the home—even when it's properly stored—doubles your risk of becoming a victim of homicide and triples the risk of suicide. Other research concludes that the presence of firearms in a house can develop into an escalation of domestic violence leading to the shooting of a family member or intimate partner.

If you insist on acquiring a gun as a means of self-defense, be sure to sign up for a gun safety course. You'll learn basic firearms safety, shooting techniques, and personal defense strategies; if you intend to carry the weapon in public, check out the requirements for obtaining a concealed-carry permit in your state.

PEPPER SPRAYS

It's not a bad idea for every Octogenarian to have access to one or more pepper spray canisters. Pepper sprays are lightweight, simple to use, and easy to carry in one's jacket, purse, or handbag. They're not expensive, so it's recommended to have several scattered around your home, in your car, and also, on your person when you go out. If you're a jogger or will be in a place that feels particularly dangerous, you can get a palm-held canister that secures with a strap that wraps across the back of your hand. The same pepper sprays used to deter human aggressors are also effective against animals such as dogs and various types of wildlife.

Police protocol says that a deterrent should match the weapon of the aggressor. This suggests that if you're confronted by an assailant wielding a gun, don't reach for pepper spray because this will most certainly escalate the situation. If the attacker is interested only in your money and uses the gun simply as a threat, once he has taken your wallet, he will just run away, leaving you unharmed. But if he sees you with the pepper spray, he may panic and shoot.

Furthermore, many types of pepper spray canisters look like guns, so the perpetrator, thinking you are armed, may not hesitate to shoot. However, if you are attacked by someone with a hand weapon such as a knife or heavy bludgeoning instrument, pepper spray is a viable deterrent.

The first decision in purchasing a pepper spray is to decide which of the three types is most suitable for your needs. The basic pepper spray shoots a mist 6 to 12 feet. (With a range of 35 feet, bear spray is the far-reaching exception.) The advantage of the spray method of delivery is that you don't have to be spot-on with your target because the spray spreads out to cover a large area. The disadvantage is that in windy situations, the spray may be blown away from your target and, in some cases, may even blow back into your own face.

The second type of pepper spray is a liquid that delivers more of a steady stream than a spray. This liquid type increases the range up to 15 feet and, when aimed correctly, is more forceful than the basic type of spray. In close quarters, such as in a car, there is a reduced risk of blow-back from a liquid spray.

The third type of pepper spray shoots a stream of liquid gel up to 20 percent farther than the standard sprays, allowing effectiveness at a greater distance between you and the perpetrator. The main advantage of the gel spray is that it sticks to the target and is not so easy to brush away. Also, the gel stream doesn't atomize like the regular pepper spray and only affects what it hits, reducing the risk of cross-contamination.

Many people think that simply buying pepper spray and storing it gives them the security they need. However, although these sprays are easy to use, it's important to understand the various steps involved in activating them. In an emergency situation, you don't want to be fumbling around trying to find the canister and wondering how to use it. It's important to practice beforehand, so when it's needed, your muscle memory can take over.

Here are the five tips in understanding how to use pepper spray. It's easy to remember because they all begin with the letter "A."

1. Awareness (Appearance) - When out in public, make yourself a "hard" target. Keep your shoulders back and walk tall in a purposeful manner as though you have a definite goal in mind. Continuously look around and stay aware of your surroundings. Don't become a "soft" target by dawdling along lost in thought or with your head down as you focus on your cell phone.

2. Access – At a time when it's needed, the pepper spray canister should be within easy access. Hook it onto a key ring or a snap-clip on a belt. Know exactly where it is when you head out. Is it in your satchel? Your purse? Your backpack? Your briefcase? At home use multiple storage locations including your bedroom, bathroom, kitchen, and within reach of the place where you sit in the evening when you read or

watch television.

3. Aim – When the would-be assailant is threatening, grab the pepper spray canister in your dominant hand and extend it out to arm's length. Have your other hand in position to push off the attacker to defend yourself. Line up your dominant eye with the top of the canister and the assailant's head, specifically the eyes. The usual range is 10 to 20 feet and is noted on the canister. Know this in advance.

4. Activate – Best to start with a practice pepper spray before stepping up to the real thing. Practice canisters, available online and in some big-box stores, are loaded with water but have the same feel and activation mechanism as the real thing. Familiarity with the grip will improve your accuracy and you'll see the distance in which the spray is effective. Furthermore, you can get used to using the canister in the dark.

With your thumb, flip up the safety switch. It's important to use your thumb instead of the index finger for two reasons. First, with all fingers wrapped around the pepper spray, you'll have a tighter grip on the canister in case the attacker tries to knock it out of your hand. Second, it's easier to aim using your thumb than the index finger. If the attacker doesn't back off, depress the trigger and hold it down for at least one second as you spray horizontally from ear to ear across the eyes, and then back and forth again one or more times as necessary. If you spray vertically up and down, not recommended, you'll likely not get the spray into both eyes.

5. Away – At this point the assailant, now disoriented, will be temporarily blinded and will start to cough and gag because breathing will become difficult. (If it makes you feel better, you should know that there are no permanent effects from any of these sprays.) Both eyes of the attacker will automatically tear up and close, and mucous will begin streaming from the nose. Nevertheless, instead of backing away, the attacker, although unable to see, will likely continue to charge. Therefore, immediately as you finish spraying, quickly get out of the line of the attack by moving away to one side. Don't just back up because you may still be within range if the attacker lunges forward. Escape in whatever direction where you see crowds of people or a safe shelter, and shout for help. *Spray, then get Away!*

TAKEAWAY FOR OCTOGENARIANS: *Remember that you have limited ability to defend yourself when* *attacked. Best advice is to stay away from places that are known to be dangerous. Next best advice is to give the attacker whatever he demands, remembering the priority is to protect yourself. Finally, equip yourself with a number of pepper sprays strategically located around your home, in your car, and within easy reach when you go out of doors. Be sure to familiarize yourself with how to use your sprays.*

ASSAULT BY CREATURES

More than one million emergency room visits and 200 deaths annually are attributable to animal encounters. However, compared with attacks by humans, serious danger from attacks by non-human creatures is rare. Animal-related deaths in controllable situations, such as on the farm or in the home, account for the majority of the deaths. Most deaths are not due to wild animals like mountain lions, wolves, bears, sharks, etc., so while it is important that people recreating in the wilderness know what to do when they encounter a potentially dangerous animal, the actual risk of death is quite low.

The rank order and frequency of attacks in the U.S. by creatures include stinging insects (hornets, bees, wasps), 30%; dogs, 20%; other crawling critters (spiders, ants, scorpions), 20%; snakes/lizards, 10%; farm animals, 10%; other mammals, reptiles and marine animals, 10%.

Animals maim or kill by biting, stinging, mauling, kicking, trampling, and goring. Kicks, stings, and bites from farm animals, insects, and dogs represent the most serious injuries and fatalities to humans. Animal attacks are rare if you don't live on a farm where horses and cattle cause 90 percent of deaths.

Despite the availability of life-saving treatment, the most lethal venomous animal encounters, accounting for an estimated 220,000 visits to the emergency department and approximately 60 deaths per year, are bee, wasp, and hornet stings and subsequent anaphylaxis. Anaphylaxis is a life-threatening allergic reaction that can occur within seconds of exposure to allergic substances. This involves hives, swelling, a sudden drop in blood pressure, and sometimes shock. People with known allergic reactions to bee stings should carry a portable epinephrine delivery device at all times and should take care to renew the medication when it expires even though the device may not have ever been used. Because insect stings are responsible for causing one-third of all annual animal-inflicted deaths, effective and affordable treatment for anaphylaxis is critical.

Ranking after stinging insects, dogs are responsible for the second-most common type of fatal animal encounter with fewer than 100 deaths annually. Although children under four years of age suffer the most fatalities, the next most vulnerable victims are persons older than 65. Around 4.5 million Americans are bitten by dogs every year, with pit bulls accounting for about half of human attacks as well as deaths by dogs. Rottweilers come second and German Shepherds third for biting incidents.

Rounding out the end of the list of deadly animals are, on average, snakes (10 deaths annually), spiders (7), bears (2), alligators (1), and sharks (1). Of little statistical significance are infrequent deaths by cougars, polar bears, wolves, and moose.

TAKEAWAY FOR OCTOGENARIANS:
Be aware of threatening situations from insects and animals in your surroundings.

ASSAULTS BY NATURAL DISASTERS

The three greatest hazards from natural disasters are, in rank order, hurricanes, floods, and fires. Hurricanes cause the most damage. Floods are most common. Fires have the greatest potential for damage because of their unpredictability, intensity, and wind factor. Recognize the likelihood of specific natural disasters occurring where you live and take steps to prepare for their occurrence.

In 2023, 2.5 million people were forced from their homes as a result of 28 natural disasters, according to data from the U.S. Census Bureau. One-third were displaced for more than a month, and one-third experienced food shortage for at least one month. In the previous year, 3.3 million people were displaced.

In 2022, the total number of deaths related to natural disaster events was around 500, but the numbers vary over a large range from year to year. Most deaths occur as a result of cyclones, hurricanes, and tornados followed by floods, wildfires, droughts, severe storms, and lightning.

***TAKEAWAY FOR OCTOGENARIANS**: Prepare for natural disasters that can occur where you live, have a plan for evacuation in case it becomes necessary, and don't be in the wrong place at the wrong time.*

Resources Consulted:

(Cohen, R. A. 2019. "Octogenarians," New York, NY: Springer) (Faircloth, U. 2020, "How to Use Pepper Spray the Right Way," Stun & Run Self Defense); (Sandorf, B., 2019, "Best Pepper Sprays: Reviews, Questions, Answers, & Top Picks," A Secure Way); (Reed, J.T., 2020, "Octogenarian's Guide to Living Longer, Happier, Healthier, & Wealthier"); (Greenlee, K., 2021, "Elder Abuse is Intolerable," National Council on Aging)

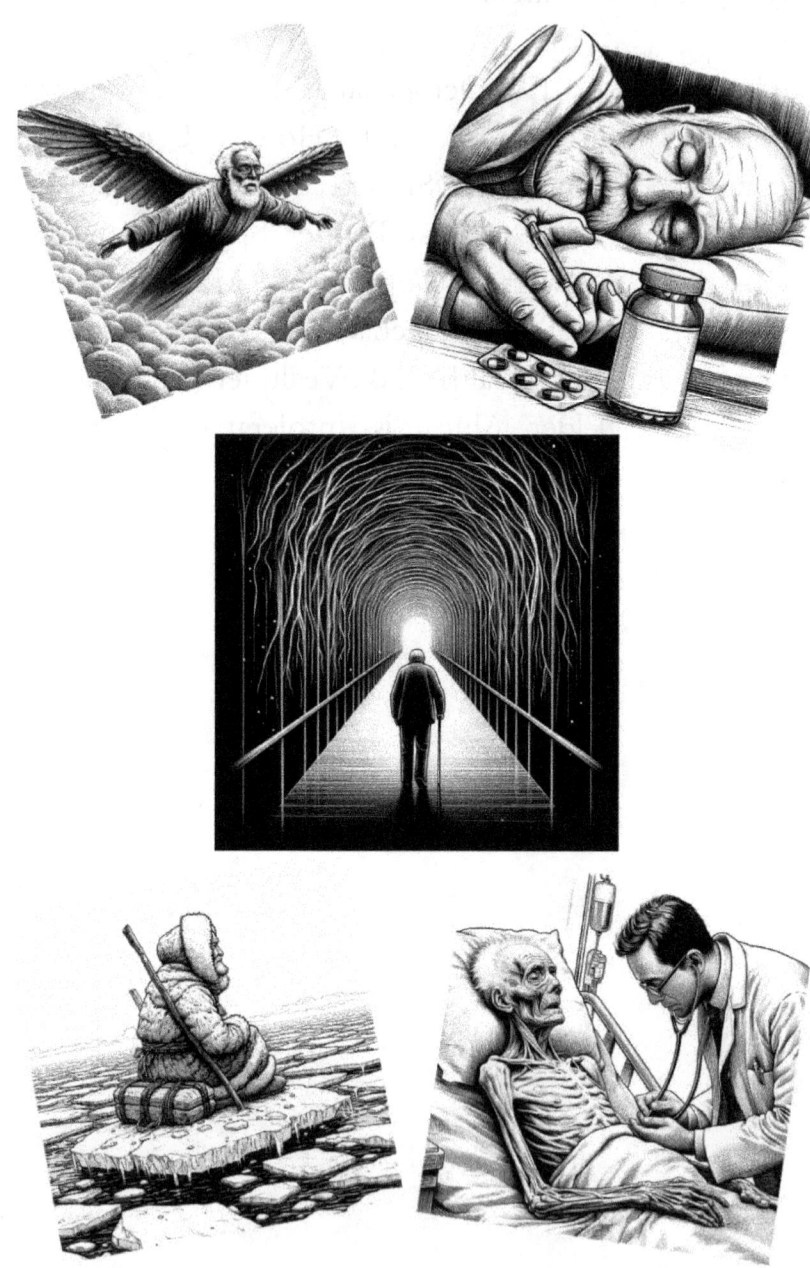

CHAPTER 6
ARRANGED

This chapter discusses the fourth of the five pathways that can lead to disability and death. This pathway also begins with an "A," and refers to being complicit in ARRANGING your own death.

AUTONOMOUS or **ASSISTED** or **ARRANGED** deaths (again, all "A's") are the 11th most frequent cause of death in America, according to the CDC. For some elderly persons with a sound reason and a supportive medical opinion, under certain circumstances arranging their own death may be their path of choice.

As reported by the CDC, in 2022, almost 50,000 Americans ended their lives either on their own or by arranging their death in states where aid-in-dying laws are in effect. An estimated 12.3 million American adults seriously thought about suicide, 3.5 million planned a suicide attempt, and 1.7 million attempted suicides unsuccessfully. The most common methods of taking one's life are by firearms, 55%; suffocation (hanging), 25%; poisoning, 12%; other, 8%.

The suicide rate for American males in 2021 was approximately four times higher than the rate for females. Males make up 50 percent of the population but commit nearly 80 percent of suicides. Suicide rates per capita vary greatly from one state to another, ranging from a high in Montana to a low in New York. Rates are generally higher in rural locales than in urban settings. Furthermore, the U.S. suicide rate has been increasing almost every year since 2000, with the greatest rate of increase among the elderly. Suicide in America is an unrecognized national crisis!

Emergency departments treat 187,000 people annually for self-harm injuries, which are usually the result of unsuccessful suicide attempts. While older adults comprise just 12 percent of the population, with more than 10,500 deaths in 2022, they make up 21 percent of suicides each year. Even if seniors initially fail their suicide attempts, they are less likely to recover from the effects because they are frailer and less likely to heal from injuries. Because elders have more access to firearms and medication, one out of four seniors who attempt to kill themselves will succeed compared to only one out of 200 youths. Seniors are often more isolated, which makes rescues difficult. Octogenarians and those who are older have the highest rate of suicides in the U.S.; ages 65 to 80 have the second highest. This is not necessarily a bad situation, as will be explained later.

People who exhibit suicidal tendencies should be given the phone number of the Suicide Crisis Hotline (988), or the National Suicide Prevention Lifeline (1-800-273-8255), or be encouraged to chat online with a trained counselor at www.suicidepreventionlifeline.org. Councilors are available 24/7 and can provide free and confidential support, crisis intervention, and referrals to local resources. Alternatively, a person may call 911 or go to the nearest Emergency Room.

Four main reasons, the so-called Four D's—Depression, Despondency, Disease, and Deliberate—each described below, account for why Octogenarians attempt suicide.

DEPRESSION

The leading cause of suicides by Octogenarians is depression. The pain of existence often becomes too much for severely depressed people to bear. An estimated 90 percent of the elderly who attempt suicide have untreated or undertreated depression. Depression is a clinical disease and is not a normal part of aging. Depression can often be cured and is just as treatable in an Octogenarian as in a younger person.

Feeling depressed is not the same as having a medical diagnosis of depression. The feeling of being depressed is an emotional state that everyone experiences from time to time, but talking with friends and family can often alleviate this feeling. Clinical depression, by contrast, is a disease that needs attention from a medical professional. People who are extremely depressed feel that nothing can relieve their pain and they consider their situation beyond hope. Feelings of profound sadness, hopelessness, and worthlessness are common among those with this diagnosis. Although most people with clinical depression don't actually commit suicide, they frequently consider it as a viable option.

What brings on depression? As senior citizens become less and less able to complete routine, daily tasks, they can easily sink into depression. If they find they have difficulty reading, seeing, hearing, driving, relating to others, or performing other activities that allow a person to remain independent or find meaning, they may feel life is no longer worth living. Signs of depression or suicidal tendencies are evident if seniors lose interest in their hobbies, isolate themselves, change their sleep routines, cry for no reason, or stop eating and drinking. In addition to feeling worthless and hopeless, they may feel abandoned and disrespected. They may talk about giving their belongings away, or they may start saying things like, "When I'm not here…".

It's important to understand that people who contemplate killing themselves are trying to get rid of their physical and emotional pain. These people may not truly want to die, but they do want to alert those around them that something is seriously wrong. Warning signs may not always be obvious, however. While some people may cry out, others keep suicidal thoughts and feelings to themselves.

Seniors need to feel connected as part of a community where they can find support, friendship, and a sense of purpose. Those who feel lonely are likely to be at higher risk of suicide. Nevertheless, because most of those who commit suicide are either living with family or are in frequent contact with family and friends, depression may be a more serious risk than loneliness in the elderly. When people die by suicide, they may have lived for a long time with a mental health condition such as depression, anxiety, or bipolar disorder.

Anyone who feels suicidal should seek medical help immediately. The family doctor may prescribe antidepressants and may make referrals to psychiatrists and therapists. It's important to make sure the people who care about you know what's going on and are there for you. Feeling connected and supported can help reduce suicide risk.

People who have survived suicide attempts have reported wanting not so much to die as to stop living so they could free themselves from emotional and/or physical pain. If some in-between state existed, some other alternative to death, many suicidal people would likely choose it instead of resorting to suicide.

TAKEAWAY FOR OCTOGENARIANS:

If you observe suicidal tendencies in yourself or others as a result of depression, it may be a clinical condition that requires medical intervention.

DESPONDENCY

Depression, which occurs as the result of a cumulation of factors over a period of time—factors such as loneliness, worthlessness, and disconnectedness from life—is a clinical disease. Despondency, on the other hand, occurs as a result of a specific loss and is characterized by deep sadness. It is not considered a disease because people avoid succumbing to a mental illness. Nonetheless, if the sense of loss is severe enough, it can lead to suicidal tendencies. Suicide as a result of despondency is often in response to an event. Not all who kill themselves do so after a long struggle with depression. Many take their own lives after sudden reversals or setbacks.

Losing a cherished one, like a spouse or a close relative, is often the most harrowing and sorrowful experience, leading to profound sadness. Additionally, relationship troubles are a significant factor in the high rates of suicide among the elderly. The dissolution of a romantic relationship is especially difficult due to the deep emotional connections, shared experiences, and joint assets that are formed over time. Thus, the end of an important relationship can bring about intense sadness. However, as the emotional turmoil of a breakup diminishes, so typically does the sadness, along with the suicidal thoughts it may have brought.

Yet, the challenge intensifies with age, as the likelihood of losing more friends and relatives increases, raising the potential for sadness.

Stanford University business school professor, Jeffrey Pfeiffer, author of "Dying for a Paycheck," looks at how management practices, including layoffs, are hurting, and in some cases, killing workers. Layoffs can kill people, literally. Losing a job has a double impact because not only does it put the individual in financial straits, but it also can have a devastating effect by diminishing one's sense of self-worth. There are also health and attitudinal consequences for managers who are laying people off, as well as for the employees who remain. Not surprisingly, layoffs increase people's stress, which can contribute to suicidal intentions.

Many seniors are living on a fixed income and may struggle to pay housing costs, medical bills, and daily living expenses. For someone who is already struggling with health issues or grief, despondency resulting from financial stress can exacerbate suicidal thoughts as an attempt to release the pressure. Studies show that the unemployed have higher suicide rates than the employed.

Suicide rates rise during economic downturns. For example, there was a spike during the Great Depression of the 1930s and also during the recession of 2008. Many elders and most Octogenarians are already retired, so stress as a result of layoffs or economic downturns is less likely to cause despondency for this demographic. An exception might be if all of an elder's retirement savings are in stocks that take a drastic downturn.

Often despondency can lead to alcohol and drug abuse, which can worsen thoughts of suicide and make people feel reckless or impulsive enough to act on their thoughts. A common risk factor of elderly suicide, accounting for one of three suicide cases, is substance abuse. Elderly persons are generally not thought of as substance abusers, but some elders may resort to using substances to self-medicate in an attempt to minimize pain. Evidence indicates that excessive drug and alcohol usage is actually prevalent among Octogenarians. Furthermore, Octogenarians can be impulsive. Under the influence of drugs and alcohol, some impulsively attempt to end their own lives, but once sobered and calmed, these people usually feel remorseful. Because high rates of drug overdose often go along with high rates of suicide, it's sometimes hard to distinguish an intentional overdose from an accidental one. Therefore, some researchers lump them together as "deaths of despair."

Declining physical health in the aged is another factor contributing to suicide. Octogenarians may no longer have the agility or strength they once had. In addition to normal aging issues with vision and hearing, there are disorders that result in chronic pain and intense physical discomfort. These conditions can bring on mobility issues that compromise quality of life and make it harder to engage in activities they enjoy. Loss of self-sufficiency often accompanies declining physical health. The more debilitating an illness, the more reliant on others elders become for care. Seniors who were once able to dress themselves, drive, read, and lead an active life may grapple with a loss of identity and the independent, vibrant person they once were. For those who have spent their lives being the strong ones taking care of others, it can be demoralizing to become reliant on others.

***TAKEAWAY FOR OCTOGENARIANS:** Despondency is a result of a major life-changing event, which may trigger suicidal tendencies; when the pain passes, so do despondency and the thoughts of taking one's life.*

DISEASE

For some, the choice to commit suicide is based on a reasoned decision often motivated by a painful terminal disease for which little to no hope of reprieve exists. Parkinson's disease, in particular, can increase suicide risk; one study found that one out of three individuals with this disease have suicidal thoughts.

Researchers discovered that while almost all serious medical conditions portend increased suicide risk, the presence of more than one disease increases suicide risk substantially. People thus afflicted aren't depressed, psychotic, maudlin, or crying out for help. They're trying to take control of their destiny and alleviate their suffering, which they believe can only be achieved by dying. They often look at their choice to commit suicide as a way to shorten a dying process that will happen regardless. Rational suicide is the reasoned taking of one's own life. However, some people judge all suicide as never being rational.

END-OF-LIFE OPTIONS

It's important to discard the stigma of the word "Suicide," which implies a type of crime similar to the word homicide, infanticide, or fratricide. When speaking of a suicide victim, the implication is that the perpetrator, namely that same person, is a criminal who has committed a crime. The illegal implication must be removed from the word and replaced by alternative terms such a "voluntary dying," "assisted dying," "death with dignity," or "aid in dying."

Words matter. Former California governor Jerry Brown, an erstwhile Jesuit priest, struggled when deciding whether to sign a bill that would permit physicians to provide lethal prescriptions to mentally competent adults who had been diagnosed with a terminal illness and faced the expectation that they would die within six months. Suicide is considered a sin by the Catholic Church and had long been deemed to be a criminal act in California and other states. But the story is that when Governor Brown considered the context as "aid-in-dying," it no longer seemed to be a criminal or sinful act but rather an act of compassion, and he signed the legislation in October 2015.

Oregon passed the nation's first aid-in-dying law. On October 27, 1997, the so-called Beaver State enacted the "Death with Dignity Act" that allows terminally ill individuals to end their lives through the voluntary, self-administration of lethal medications expressly prescribed by a physician for that purpose. After a lawsuit was filed in 2021 challenging the residency requirement in the law, the residency requirement was removed in July 2023, opening the door for any U.S. citizen to avail themselves of the law.

In 2022, 146 physicians in Oregon wrote prescriptions for 431 people to receive the lethal medications under the Act. That year 278 died from ingesting the prescribed medications, including 32 who had received prescriptions in previous years. Eighty-five percent of these patients were over 65 years of age, and more than half were Octogenarians. The most common diagnoses were cancer, 64%; heart disease, 12%; and neurological ailments, 10%. The most frequently reported end-of-life concerns were inability to participate in activities that made life enjoyable, loss of autonomy, loss of dignity, burden on caregivers, loss of control over bodily functions, and uncontrollable pain.

In other states with end-of-life laws, the patient must be at least 18, have a terminal disease with less than six months to live, and have the mental capacity to request aid in dying. These states have protections that include waiting periods and require qualifications for attending healthcare providers. The second state to pass a similar law was Washington with the "Death with Dignity Act" in 2008. Montana followed in 2009 with its "Rights of the Terminally Ill Act." Other states and districts that have passed end-of-life legislation include Vermont (2013), Colorado (2016), District of Columbia (2016), Hawaii (2019), New Jersey (2019), Maine (2019), and New Mexico (2021). Another dozen states have similar legislation under consideration.

End of Life options are only for physical terminal illnesses, not for dementia. Dementia is not a disease; it's a syndrome that can lead to any number of diseases that are fatal. Dementia patients can be physically active for many years and with a caregiver nearby, can integrate within public settings. Although they may have mood swings, often they are happy, particularly those with Frontotemporal Dementia (FTD). Whatever their situation, they are in no position to make a decision about an end-of-life option.

TAKEAWAY FOR OCTOGENARIANS:
If end-of-life options are a consideration for yourself or other loved ones, check out the laws in your state and consult a medical professional.

EUTHANASIA

Assisted or arranged suicide is not the same as euthanasia, although the two phrases are often used interchangeably. Euthanasia involves the administration of a lethal agent by another person to a patient, meaning the person performing the euthanasia, often a medical doctor, is directly responsible for ending the patient's life. In physician-assisted suicide, the patient must self-administer the medications provided by a physician. The patient decides whether and when to ingest the lethal medication.

Euthanasia is illegal in most of the world's countries and can even result in a murder conviction for the administering physician. However, a small but growing number of countries have legalized euthanasia in certain extreme cases that must meet stringent conditions. In most countries where euthanasia is legal, the patient must be suffering from a terminal illness with no hope of recovery and must be in significant pain. Moreover, the administering physician must have nothing to gain from the patient's death. In countries that permit euthanasia, a doctor is allowed by law to end a person's life by painless means, as long as the person and their family agree.

Euthanasia can be either passive, in which medical efforts to prolong the patient's life are terminated and the disease is allowed to take its course, or active, in which the physician triggers death by prescribing and/or administering a lethal dose of medication. All the states and District of Columbia mentioned above with right-to-die laws allow passive euthanasia, but active euthanasia remains prohibited throughout the entire U.S. Active euthanasia is more controversial and is likely to involve religious, moral, ethical, legal, and compassionate arguments.

To be legal, euthanasia must be voluntary, meaning the patient agrees to, and most likely requests, the procedure. If the patient cannot give consent, such as with infants or incapacitated individuals, the procedure is classified as non-voluntary euthanasia and is considered to be murder in most countries. Eight countries have enacted laws that allow euthanasia. Netherlands was the first (2001). Others include Belgium (2002), Luxembourg (2009), Canada (2016), Australia (2019), New Zealand (2019), Columbia (2021), and Spain (2021).

Euthanasia is legal in the Netherlands under specific conditions. The attending physician carries out the euthanasia by administering a fatal dose of a suitable drug to the patient upon his or her expressed request. In February 2024, the issue of euthanasia made world headlines when a Catholic former Dutch prime minister died by euthanasia, hand in hand with his wife. They were both 93. Their deaths were part of a growing trend in the Netherlands for "duo euthanasia."

Although still rare, in the first three years since euthanasia became legal, 58 people in the Netherlands were granted euthanasia at the same time as their partners.

TAKEAWAY FOR OCTOGENARIANS: Euthanasia is complicated and generally illegal. Check the laws carefully in your jurisdiction if this is a consideration.

VSED

If not now, then when? Whether or not a state has a death-with-dignity statute, there are other options to hasten one's death on your own terms with no outside medical involvement, options that are legal in every state. As an alternative to physical-assisted suicide, a patient has the right to refuse food and fluids, known as Voluntarily Stopping Eating and Drinking (VSED), even if doing so will cause the patient to die. Do it on your own terms by stopping food, water, and medications except for pain relief.

If conducted at home, this process can be carried out privately without anyone other than the patient involved. In a medical setting, VSED can proceed with a physician's knowledge, although there are ethical and legal uncertainties about the physician's involvement. While the physician may make the patient comfortable when undertaking VSED, physician involvement is not a form of assisted suicide.

One can live for a long time without eating—in some cases up to four or more weeks—but dehydration speeds up the dying process. Death from VSED can occur within a time span from a few days up to a number of weeks depending upon age, fitness, and illness of the patient. People who begin this process often express a sense of peace, and describe a feeling of euphoria or pleasant lightheadedness. Discomfort can be alleviated with mild sedatives or mouth swabs. Palliative sedation is an ethical and legal end-of-life option, but it is up to the medical provider to determine if it is appropriate. After a few days, energy levels will decrease, and the patient will become less mentally alert and sleepier. By the end of the first week, most people pass in and out of consciousness until they ultimately become unarousable. Stopping medications, except for pain relief, may speed up the process.

TAKEAWAY FOR OCTOGENARIANS:
An advantage of VSED is that people may change their minds anytime… and simply order a beer and a burger. VSED is what humans have done for millennia when they reached the right moment for it.

DELIBERATE

For the sake of completeness, listed below are other deliberate reasons people seek to end their lives:

- Suicides among a group can sometimes be performed under social pressure when members relinquish autonomy to a leader.
- Suicide bombers such as Japanese Kamikaze pilots or religious extremists carry out their missions as a duty to a higher cause or moral obligation.
- Suicides such as self-immolations can be carried out as a protest to a perceived injustice.
- Suicides can be an attempt to inflict guilt on someone.
- Suicides can be a response to bullying and abuse.
- Suicides can be part of a murder-suicide arrangement when one or both partners decide to die together.
- Suicides can be caused by shame and humiliation resulting from allegations of sexual or criminal misconduct.
- Suicides, in some cultures, can be an altruistic gesture considered an act of respect, courage, and wisdom, such as when elders end their lives to leave greater amounts of food for younger people.
- Suicides, called honor suicides, can occur in some societies in which a person's actions have dishonored their family or clan.

• Suicides can be carried out as a consequence of a genetic link to a family history of suicide.

• Suicides, sometimes called "suicide by cop," can occur when mass shooters, who are often mentally deranged, go on killing rampages with the intention that they will be taken down by the police or security forces.

WHERE TO GET HELP

A universal dialing code launched in July 2022 is broadening access to lifesaving suicide prevention and crisis services. Dialing 988 connects people in crisis directly to the Suicide & Crisis Lifeline, where counselors provide free, unbiased, and confidential support 24/7. Located in 200 crisis centers all over the country, these counselors are experienced in responding to people in emotional distress, including those with suicidal intent. Dialing 988 is just like dialing 911 for emergency response or 411 for information services. There's no need to dial any other digits besides those three. Older adults won't get a busy signal, nor will they be put on hold. Help will be immediately available.

Text HOME to 741741 to reach a trained crisis counselor through the Crisis Text Line, a global not-for-profit organization, that's free, 24/7, and confidential.

U.S. veterans or service members in crisis can call 988 and then press 1, or text 838255 to reach the Veterans Crisis Line and speak with a responder trained in crisis intervention and military culture. Or chat using veteranscrisisline.net/get-help-now/chat/.

The Institute on Aging runs the Friendship Line (800-971-0016) created exclusively for seniors and people with disabilities.

Resources Consulted:

(CDC, 2023, "Saving Lives, Protecting People"); (Robinson L. et al, Help Guide, 2021, "Depression in Older Adults: Signs, Symptoms, Treatment"); (Reger, M.A. et al, 2020, "Suicide Mortality and Coronavirus Disease 2019—A Perfect Storm?" JAMA Psychiatry); (Cherry, K., 2020, "Moderate Depression: Symptoms, Treatment, and Coping," Very Well Mind); (Serani, D., 2019, "Suicide Prevention in Older Adults." Psychology Today); (Smith, J., 2022, "Suicide Among Seniors: Causes, Prevention, and Treatment," ABC Press); (Reed, J.T., 2020, "Octogenarian's Guide to Living Longer, Happier, Healthier, & Wealthier," www.jtreed.com); (Clarke, J., 2023, "How the Five Stages of Grief Can Help Process a Loss," Very Well Mind); (Pfeiffer, J., 2018, "Dying for a Paycheck," Harper Business); (Wasmer, L., 2000, "Depression: What It Is, How to Beat It," Enslow Publishers); (Battin, M.P. et al, 1998, "Physician Assisted Suicide: Expanding the Debate," Journal of Medical Ethics)

CHAPTER 7
AGING

Here we come to the last of the five ways of dying, and for most people, the preferred way to pass on: simply by AGING.

What does it mean to die simply by aging? The phenomenon of dying in this manner is not well understood by the medical community. The body's organs simply wear out, and as one of them fails, the others begin to shut down as well. Finally, everything in the body is worn out. Although the dying person may experience the usual stiffness in joints and aches that seniors become accustomed to over previous decades, this final fading away occurs without pain, disease, or injury.

But instead of focusing on dying, better to prioritize healthy aging. Healthy aging implies maintaining adequate physical abilities and a clear mind with perhaps only minimal confusion, stress, and forgetfulness. Although you may be moving more slowly, you still have sufficient mobility to perform the five daily activities essential to caring for your body: grooming; dressing; ambulating; shopping; and eating. According to a National Health Interview Survey, more than 20 percent of adults older than 85 years require assistance with these daily activities.

LONGEVITY VS LIFESPAN

Aging in humans is a complex process that requires us to differentiate between two concepts: longevity and lifespan. Longevity refers to the average number of years we live, which is around the mid to high 70s statistically. But lifespan is not the same. Nobody reaches the full natural lifespan, which is estimated, by people who seem to know about these things, to be between 130 and 135 years, the age we could theoretically achieve if we were to encounter no diseases, injuries, accidents, or harmful environmental factors during the span of our entire life. In other words, lifespan is the time we could live until we eventually die by simply aging.

Modern medicine and better living standards have gradually reduced the gap between longevity and lifespan. In 1800, the average life expectancy in the U.S. was somewhere between 30 to 40 years. In 1960 it rose to 52.2 years. In 2021, life expectancy at birth was 76.4 years—a drop from 77.0 years in 2020, mainly due to COVID-19. For males, life expectancy fell 0.7 years from 74.2 in 2020 to 73.5 in 2021. For females, life expectancy fell 0.6 years from 79.9 in 2020 to 79.3 in 2021. Studies show that genetics are about 25 percent responsible for longevity, so pick your parents and grandparents carefully!

EVOLUTIONARY BIOLOGY

According to evolutionary biology, humans are among the few organisms on the planet that live beyond their reproductive age, whereas most species perish as soon as they lose their reproductive ability. It makes sense that in case we don't die by other causes, aging can cause death in order to prevent humans from becoming too numerous. Aging may just be the body's reaction to the fact that we are no longer able to reproduce. Only the strongest, meaning those who have adapted best to the challenges and changes of living in this world, survive, and that applies to us as Octogenarians.

It seems contradictory that, except for the aging stage of life, people enjoy anticipating all the other stages. Youngsters are eager to become teenagers. Young boys look forward to the day they can start shaving, growing a beard, driving a car, and speaking in deeper voices. Young girls are excited as their breasts start growing and when they are old enough to wear makeup and high-heeled shoes.

When we become young adults, we want to leave behind the years of study in schools and colleges as we look forward to finding a job. When our careers progress, we are hoping to become a partner in a firm or get the promotion that earns us the corner office. And after a 45-year career, we look forward to retiring so we can spend more time on hobbies, family, traveling, or other interests. But at the first signs of aging, which show as changes in our skin and hair, we do whatever we can to reverse the age clock.

To develop a healthy attitude about growing into our 70s and 80s, we first need to understand the steps that lead to aging. The following sections examine how individual parts of the human body change as they age, and what we can do to keep them viable and functional. I am indebted to John J. Medina, a molecular biologist and medical research scientist, and to his book "The Clock of Ages," first published in 1987 by Cambridge University Press, which gives the following tour of the aging human body.

SKIN & HAIR

The aging process starts with changes in the three top layers of the skin—the epidermis, dermis, and hypodermis. As years go by, every layer of the skin is affected as it undergoes dramatic changes, the source of the most obvious external signs of aging.

As our body's largest organ, the skin is our first line of defense against harmful bacteria, viruses, pollution, and chemicals all around us in the outside world. Skin regulates body temperature, maintains fluid balance, controls moisture loss, recognizes pain sensations, protects against the sun's harmful ultraviolet rays, and absorbs shocks. Not only does skin hold everything in, but it also plays a crucial role by providing an airtight, watertight, and flexible barrier between the outside world and the regulated systems within the body.

In many ways, the skin is unique because as an outward highly visible organ, in states of both disease and health it commands a great deal of attention. Glowing, clear, younger, fresher skin is highly sought after in our society.

The extent of exposure to the elements, particularly

the sun, is the primary factor that determines skin deterioration. The cells in our skin stop functioning for various reasons and eventually die, which impairs the function of the tissue in which they reside. When enough skin tissue becomes damaged, we see changes in our skin's appearance—unwanted changes such as wrinkles, creases, and furrows. Age spots, cellulite, varicose veins, moles, and age tags appear in increasing numbers. The skin also becomes dry and leathery. As a result of muscle mass loss and decreased skin resilience, sagging pockets of skin develop under the eyes, beneath the upper arms, and below the chin. Other effects include broadening and lengthening of the nose and ears.

Changes in the hair due to cellular deterioration of the hair follicles are a second obvious sign of aging. As gray and white hair emerges, hair loses luster, and thinning occurs. Hairlines recede, and baldness may develop.

The changes brought about by aging cannot be controlled by humans, but that has not stopped us from trying. Attempts to reverse or cover up the signs of aging by seeking to alter the natural biology of the skin's three layers have led to the creation of the multi-billion-dollar beauty products and hair-care industries that entice with prospects of miraculous results.

Thousands of anti-aging products offered by the cosmetic and pharmaceutical industries claim to reverse the natural effects that become evident when skin begins to lose elasticity and develop fine lines. Skin moisturizers, the most common product, hydrate the top layer of skin cells and seal in moisture. Collagen, the most abundant protein in the body, is one of the most popular supplements on the market. Collagen reputedly improves the skin's appearance, while also strengthening nails, keeping bones and joints healthy, and building muscle mass that promotes balanced metabolism and healthy weight. The human body requires 20 different amino acids, which are typically contained in collagen supplements.

Some people may have specific skin issues that they want to address with extra products. For instance, chemical exfoliants are products that peel off the old layer of skin cells and reveal the new layers of skin underneath. The cosmetic industry offers an array of treatments such as Botox, fillers, chin-shaping, lip augmentation, hair regrowth, and facial renewal. However, regardless of how much money and effort is expended to reverse the natural process of aging, in the long term it's a losing battle.

For those who define who they are as a person based on their appearance, aging can be depressing. Physical ailments, and in the extreme, even suicide, can result from depression. By the time people reach old age, if they have any self-awareness, they should know that their identity is not their appearance. They are still the same person they always were!

Although various products and procedures may improve the skin's health and appearance to some extent for a period of time, using beauty products and treatments does not necessarily mean that one is better off than those who ignore the cosmetic ads and embrace the natural aging process.

There is a positive way to view the age-related changes in the body's appearance. First, it is important to remember that these changes in appearance do not affect the body's inward functioning. All the body's systems and processes work normally and are not harmed by how one looks. The digestive system, the heart, the blood circulation, and the breathing all continue to function. Nor do age-related outward changes affect a person's physical abilities, their attitude towards life, their intelligence, their hobbies, and their ability to enjoy the world through their senses.

There are more than 3,000 different skin afflictions, but only one of them is a major threat to life. It is melanoma, a skin cancer that can spread to other organs. The skin protects itself from the sun's UV rays by producing melanin, but this is not enough when people spend a lot of time outdoors in the sun. People of all ages should use sunscreen with at least 40 SPF.

SPF (Sun Protection Factor) indicates how long the sunscreen will allow you to stay in the sun without getting burned, compared to how long it will take to burn without that particular sunscreen. For example, if you usually burn in 15 minutes without sunscreen and you use a sunscreen rated SPF 10, you should be able to stay in the sun for 10 times longer (2.5 hours longer) without burning.

TAKEAWAY FOR OCTOGENARIANS:

If you want to keep treatments simple, you need only three products for basic skin care: a gentle face wash, a moisturizer with amino acids, and a sunscreen with at least 40 SPF. Most importantly, visit your dermatologist at least once a year for a full-body skin check in order to identify and remove any developing skin cancers and to have those pesky precancerous skin lesions removed as well.

MUSCULOSKELETAL SYSTEM

As our skin changes, we also experience changes in the joints, muscles, bones, tendons, and ligaments—changes that can affect our movement. While skin gives us external flexibility and protection from the environment, skeletal structure provides internal support and stability. Bones, our internal framework, are made of cells, blood vessels, water, and minerals consisting mainly of calcium and also lead, zinc, and potassium. Bones are constantly renewing themselves, so the human skeleton is replaced about once every seven years. But with age, our cells lose the ability to regenerate. Calcium is reduced, and the bones become weaker, porous, and more fragile, making them prone to break, especially if we fall.

People on average lose about five percent of their bone weight per decade starting in their 40s, but the rate gradually increases to the point that for Octogenarians, the loss can reach up to 30 percent in total. The best way to keep our bones strong is to add calcium to our diets and to follow a healthy diet with regular exercise.

Contrary to what many people believe, loss of mobility is not caused by problems with our bones but by problems with our joints where bones meet and are connected by ligaments (bone to bone), tendons (muscle to bone), cartilage (protective layer at the end of bones), and synovial fluid (lubricating fluid between the joints). As we age, all these parts start to wear out. Ligaments and tendons tend to break and become less flexible, resilient, and elastic. Cartilage also changes as it becomes thinner and provides less cushioning between bones as they move.

These changes result in stiffness that causes more difficulty in movement and consequently makes older people more likely to get injured. Muscles keep most of their strength, losing only 10 – 20 percent, until our 70s. But for Octogenarians, the loss of muscle mass is typically 30 to 40 percent of the total. Loss is greater in the lower body than in the upper body, which is why Octogenarians often have to use their hands and arms in addition to legs to get up from a sitting position or from the floor.

As with many biological processes, if muscles are not used, they will start to shrink. The most important function of the joints, bones, and muscles is to enable us to walk, which is usually a smooth and steady motion. If this walking movement is no longer smooth but becomes a shaky gait, also called an ataxic gait, Octogenarians risk falling. For this reason, they should seek physical therapy for gait improvement.

TAKEAWAY FOR OCTOGENARIANS:
Don't neglect your mobility. Take calcium supplements as advised by your doctor; exercise regularly; stay hydrated; get enough sleep; and follow the old saying, "Use it or lose it."

NEUROLOGICAL AGING

One of the biggest worries as we age is loss of our mental abilities. As we get older, the brain diminishes in size and becomes more filled with fluid. By the time we are 65, almost 10 percent of the brain cells we had as young adults have vanished and there is no renewal. From our adolescence to the time we become Octogenarians, the brain loses weight, typically about 5 to 10 percent of its mass, which correlates with the loss of brain cells.

The first sign of aging of the brain usually shows up as memory difficulties in the form of brief memory gaps, failure to remember things in the moment. We might often forget the names of people we have known for a long time or struggle to recall the words for familiar things in our life such as what to call an orange or the name of a particular flower.

A related issue is having a clear sense of a fact, but

not being able to remember what that fact is. Often when we can't remember something, we ignore it for a while only to have it pop up in our mind at a later time when we're busy with some other unrelated activity. This is not a memory problem, because the word you're looking for is still stored somewhere in the brain. This is a problem of retrieval. Somehow the ability to quickly recall something is reduced as we age.

A useful technique to activate the retrieval part of the mind is to use an alphabet recital. For example, if you can't think of the name of a specific tree, start by picturing the tree in your mind. Then begin with "A" and slowly mentally go through the alphabet while keeping an image of the tree in your awareness. Suddenly, when you reach "O," the retrieval function may work as the word "oak" pops into your mind, and you have the word you were trying to recall. If this method doesn't succeed the first time, repeat the process by going through the alphabet again.

Another technique is to go through the alphabet looking for the first two consonants together in a word that make a single distinct sound, called a consonant blend or a consonant digraph. Common digraphs include "ch" as in "change," "chill," or "chapter." In searching for the name of a tree that you're picturing, the retrieval mechanism may suddenly activate as the word "cherry tree" pops up in your memory.

To illustrate this memory-lapse issue, there's a story about two businessmen having lunch together at a restaurant. One of the two businessmen spots an old friend entering the establishment who begins walking toward their table. For the life of him, the seated man can't remember the name of his friend who is moving ever closer and closer. Then, at the very last moment, he finally recalls his friend's name, but when he turns to introduce the two, he suddenly forgets the name of his luncheon partner!

Sleep is another issue that accompanies aging of the brain. Because sleep is essential for brain repair and consolidation of memories, sleep deprivation can accelerate brain aging. Sleep problems also impact our motor functions, which tend to be affected by the dying of cells and fibers in the brain. We may not be able to move as fast, maintain balance, or control muscles that coordinate our movements. When we sleep, our brains remove toxins and repair damage that occurred during the day. Sleep also consolidates memories, which helps us learn and remember new information. As a restorative function, sleep is essential for renewing energy and refreshing ourselves for the next day.

Throughout life, the number of hours we sleep gradually decreases from 20 hours a day as babies to nine hours as teens, seven hours as adults, then down to five hours per night after the age of 65. However, by this age we often add another hour or so with afternoon naps. As Octogenarians, we tend not to be able to sleep for long periods, often awakening multiple times throughout the night with difficulty falling asleep again. As much as 20 percent of the night may be restless rather than restful. A night of uninterrupted sleep becomes rare.

Three techniques can potentially help to overcome these problems. First, your family doctor may prescribe sleeping pills, a simple and direct way to ensure you get a full night's deep sleep. A second approach is to adopt an ancient meditation technique while lying in bed waiting for sleep to take over. Begin by trying to stop the activity of your mind by not thinking about anything. Then, as you lie there, focus your attention on the tip of your nose or close your eyes and "watch" your breath as it goes in and out of your body. When you find yourself suddenly thinking about something, stop and refocus on your breath. The third approach, if you find yourself tossing and turning for half an hour or so, don't try to resist. Turn on the light and pick up a book or magazine to read for, say, 20 minutes before returning to bed. Perhaps not appropriate to mention here, but after a romp with your partner, you may simply drift off to sleep with a smile.

Additional sleep-enhancing measures that help many people, include: engaging in exercise during the day to alleviate stress and tire the body; avoiding screen time on the TV, cell phone, and computer before going to bed; using a white-noise machine; wearing a sleep mask; taking a shower or reading for a while; and maintaining a consistent bedtime and wake-time schedule.

TAKEAWAY FOR OCTOGENARIANS:
You already know the basics for staving off neurological aging, such as exercising daily, eating a healthy diet, getting an adequate amount of sleep, and drinking plenty of water. In addition, create a daily routine of exercising the brain by such activities as engaging in Sudoku challenges, playing Kakuro games, solving crossword puzzles, learning a foreign language, or pursuing other exercises that stimulate the brain.

To further improve your brain health, take a walk. There's evidence that walking, especially outdoors, is great medicine for the mind. Walking can help grow new brain cells, boost creativity, enhance one's mood, reduce risk of cognitive decline, and reduce stress.

HEART, LUNGS, & VASCULATURE

As an Octogenarian, you will have become familiar with the medical terms related to the heart: atriums, ventricles, aortas, vasculature, ejection fraction, sinus rhythm, and more. And you will have learned the terms describing problems that often affect the heart: atrial fibrillation, heart flutter, tachycardia, congestive heart disease, aortic atherosclerosis, arrhythmias, endocarditis, and so on. Finally, you will know the various heart medications like metoprolol, digoxin, warfarin, and Eliquis, as well as medical procedures such as cardioversion and ablation. If you don't know these terms you probably will soon from your cardiologist, because heart problems, which are common among the elderly, can arise that change the heart's rhythm in a way that it doesn't function as well and may not be able to pump enough blood to meet the body's demands.

In addition to being arguably the most vital organ in the body, the heart is the only organ that can cause immediate death if it stops. When other organs start to fail, they take some time before they cease working completely. The good news, however, is that several home diagnostic devices can be used any time of the day to monitor the heart's functions and to alert you early to the onset of any pending problems.

Some worsening aspects of the aging of the heart, such as a decrease in heart rate and reduction in the amount of oxygen you take in with each breath, can be corrected with interventions. The main way to reverse deterioration of the cardiovascular system is by altering your lifestyle—mainly changes in diet and exercise.

As compared to the aerobic capacity of a young adult, by age 65 we have lost 30 to 40 percent of our aerobic power, which measures the body's ability to power our muscles using oxygen from the heart and lungs. The heart undergoes a decrease in its rate of pumping as well as in the volume of blood it pumps as we age. In addition, stiffness and decreased elasticity of the arteries cause increased resistance to blood flow in the vasculature, and the arteries become blocked with cholesterols, triglycerides, and lipoproteins.

Lungs also lose their efficiency as we age. Adults average 12 - 20 breaths per minute, whereas Octogenarians show a wider range of 10 to 30 breaths per minute as a result of alcohol, medications, sleep apnea, and other medical disorders. As we age, the lungs draw in less oxygen from the air, which means less oxygenated blood cells reach our tissues, leaving us less energized with weakened muscles. As Octogenarians, our previous oxygen-to-tissue transfer rate has been halved.

TAKEAWAY FOR OCTOGENARIANS:
Every Octogenarian should have two critical home diagnostic devices to monitor the heart. First, it would be smart to have a Smart Watch that can measure blood oxygen levels and heart rate throughout the day whether at rest or during active exercise. The typical range should be between 50 and 100 beats per minute. The watch can also indicate if you are in sinus (normal) rhythm or atrial fibrillation. If you find yourself with A-Fib for any extended period of time, it's time to see a cardiologist. The other home medical device is a blood pressure monitor to keep track of the pressure variations during the day. Ideal is 120 systolic and 80 diastolic, normally written as 120/80 mm Hg.

GASTROINTESTINAL SYSTEM

The digestive system's organs are quite resilient and can last well into our 90s, even though they decline a bit as we get older. The salivary glands, which are the first part of the digestive system, produce less saliva, making our mouths drier and our taste duller as we age. The stomach also produces less gastric juice, and we have only about 75 percent of what we had in our middle age than what we have in our 80s. Although this makes it harder to break down meat, the stomach still works well. The small intestines, together with the liver and pancreas, digest food, and generally keep working well into old age, but they have more trouble absorbing some nutrients like calcium. That's why elders may need supplements like Vitamin B12, D, and calcium.

The large intestines and the kidneys are responsible for ridding the body of waste after nutrients have been extracted. The colon makes the waste solid and dry by taking out fluids. Even though there are many ads for constipation relief, there is no proof that aging causes this problem. The colon does its job well in our later years. A sedentary lifestyle can "plug up the works" but maintaining a level of activity helps to keep things moving. However, we should still get regular colorectal exams to check for signs of colon cancer.

The kidneys are the part of the digestive system most affected by aging. They filter the blood and remove the waste products, but they get smaller and lighter as we age, and their vessels get stiffer and narrower. This means that they are not as efficient at cleaning the blood. We can lose half of the filtering ability we had as young adults by the time we are in our 80s. This can lead to uremic poisoning by which the kidneys fail to filter out the nitrogen waste products. Too much nitrogen in the blood is toxic to the body.

The bladder also changes with age. It can't hold as much urine or empty as well as before. Another issue is that young adults feel the urge to go when their bladders are only half full, but elders don't feel it until the bladder is almost full, so they have less time to react. The prostate gland in men enlarges with age to the point that medical intervention may be needed.

TAKEAWAY FOR OCTOGENARIANS:
To maintain a healthy efficient gastrointestinal system, be mindful of the need for vitamin and mineral supplements and digestive aids. Avoid foods that upset your stomach or are hard to digest.

If incontinence is an issue, always know the location of the closest bathroom. If you are not sure you can trust your system's timing, you may want to consider adult diapers and other products for incontinence.

HOW THE SENSES AGE

As we get older, our five senses—vision, hearing,

smell, taste, and touch—lose some of their function, but this does not affect the body's and mind's resiliency or our ability to handle the daily activities of life. Moreover, there are many medical treatments and devices that can help fix or reduce any sensory problems that do arise.

When we are in our 80s, our eyes change and the pupils become smaller, which means less light can enter, so we need more light to read. The eye also takes longer to adapt to different levels of light, which makes driving at night harder with the bright lights from oncoming cars. We also start to lose our near vision and become more far-sighted around age 40. Fortunately, many of the common eye problems—such as Astigmatism, Cataracts, Glaucoma, Macular Degeneration, Lazy Eye—can be treated with glasses, medicine, or surgery.

Our ears sag and grow bigger with age, but this does not affect our hearing. Too much ear wax can make hearing worse, but putting oil drops in the ears periodically during the year can solve this problem. Aging usually causes loss of high-pitched sounds, so one solution is asking people to speak louder or lower the pitch of their voices. Hearing aids, TV adapters, and other devices are also options.

The senses of taste and smell are connected, and they mostly work well for older people into their 80s. Taste buds die as we age but they quickly grow back, which lets us enjoy the same variety of tastes we had previously. Likewise, our sense of smell stays strong as we get older.

The sense of touch lets us feel pressure, pain, and temperature. Unlike the other senses, touch is not limited to a single site and can be felt by many parts of the body. People of all ages need physical contact and the soothing touch of others, to stay healthy.

TAKEAWAY FOR OCTOGENARIANS:
In general, the senses for people in their 80s are a bit weaker, which means they need better lighting, louder sounds, stronger smells, spicier foods, and more stimulation to feel sensation. But the condition of the senses does not typically have an impact on one's mental and physical abilities. Vision and hearing are the two senses that are most affected by aging, but most problems can be fixed by glasses, hearing aids, caption phones, other speech-to-readout devices, and medical treatment. Get a medical check-up at least once a year for your hearing and vision. Place reading glasses throughout your home—living room, bedroom, kitchen, office, and bathroom—so a pair is always at hand and you won't have to search for them all the time.

REPRODUCTIVE SYSTEM

Humans are different from most living things because they live longer than they can reproduce. It is also strange that they still want to have sex in their later years even though they can't have children anymore. Instead of wondering why this happens, elders should just have fun with it as long as they can.

Another thing that is different about humans is that women go through menopause and stop being able to have children, which is something that happens only to a few mammals. But menopause in women does not necessarily lower their desire for sex. Surveys suggest that many women in their 80s say they enjoy active sex lives, but they need to be careful because their reproductive organs get dry and more sensitive.

As men get older, they may have difficulty in getting and keeping an erection. Like women, they may need more time to get aroused than they did when younger, but they still enjoy sex. Luckily, there are many things that can help both men and women with their interest in sex, such as erotic toys and devices as well as medical treatments and drugs like Sildenafil (Viagra).

TAKEAWAY FOR OCTOGENARIANS:
Sex interest and activity for both men and women do not always

decrease with age. It doesn't matter if they have sex or not, because it doesn't change their mental or physical abilities.

DYING OF OLD AGE

The phrase, "dying of old age," is commonly used to describe the passing of an elderly person when the specific cause isn't clear. In medical terms, old age itself isn't a cause of death. Rather, as individuals grow older, they're more prone to various health issues, and their bodies may not recover as well from certain stresses. Death in the elderly often results from a mix of declining bodily functions and chronic health conditions.

For instance, in the later stages of life, one's metabolism and appetite might decrease, leading to less food and water intake. Energy levels typically drop, and the tendency to nap becomes more frequent. There's also a likelihood to become less engaged in social activities and to concentrate on a smaller circle of people and interests.

The oldest person ever recorded, whose age has been verified, lived to the age of 122 ½ years. Other claims of individuals who reportedly died at the age of 135 or 134, have not been independently confirmed due to the lack of reliable birth records. But the issue is not the number of years lived, but rather the years with quality of life, which is most certainly fewer. At least, for now!

Resources Consulted:

(Medina, J.J., 1987, "The Clock of Ages: Why We Age, How We Age, Winding Back the Clock," Cambridge University Press); (Kahn, R.K., Rowe, J.W., 1998, "The Octogenarian's Guide to Living Longer and Better," MacArthur Foundation); (Zweigenhaft, R.L., 2017, "The Octogenarian's Online Guide to Health," Macmillan Learning Press); (Benedetti, J. "Effects of Aging on the Skin," 2024, Healthy Aging; Harvard Medical School, Merck Manuals)

CHAPTER 8
A FINAL WORD

There are fundamentally only five ways one might pass away—by an Accident, Ailment, Assault, Arrangement, or simply Aging. It's important for Octogenarians to be mindful of these ways and to take steps to try to avoid what they feel to be, for themselves, the less favorable outcomes.

Delving into the topic of trying to control our demise is complex. Various elements, including our genetic makeup, lifestyle choices, environmental exposure, health conditions, unforeseen events, and personal decisions, can all play a role in shaping when and how we depart from this life. Some of these aspects are manageable, while others are beyond our control.

Consider our health, for instance. We have the power to influence it positively by maintaining a balanced diet, engaging in regular physical activity, refraining from smoking, limiting alcohol consumption, and keeping up with health check-ups and screenings. Such measures can diminish the likelihood of experiencing certain adverse medical conditions, thus potentially extending our longevity.

On the flip side, factors such as inherited health risks, spontaneous genetic changes, or certain pervasive environmental pollutants are beyond our ability to control. These sorts of factors can elevate the risk of health problems that may potentially reduce our longevity.

When it comes to our safety, we have the ability to make choices that minimize danger—choices such as obeying traffic laws, using seat belts and helmets, and avoiding risky behaviors. Taking these kinds of precautions can reduce our chances of involvement in fatal accidents or incurring injuries. Yet, there are unpredictable elements—for instance other people's actions, weather anomalies, or natural calamities—that we can't control, which could increase the risk of accidental death.

We can, nevertheless, exert some influence over our end-of-life care by documenting our healthcare preferences in advance directives and living wills, and by appointing healthcare proxies. Taking these steps can help to ensure our care aligns with our desires by clearly defining what interventions we do and do not want. Despite these measures, however, factors like the healthcare system's capabilities, healthcare providers' decisions, and legal regulations can impact the care we receive, sometimes in ways we might not prefer.

So, is it possible to control the circumstances of our passing? The answer isn't straightforward. It hinges on our definition of control and on how we weigh the controllable versus the uncontrollable factors. In the end, while we might have some sway over the process, absolute control is something that eludes us.

It's a bit of a shock when we, as Octogenarians, realize that statistically speaking, only 10 to 15 percent of our life remains ahead of us. Sure, in recent years the mirror has reflected noticeable indications of aging on our faces and our bodies. We also have been keenly aware of the aches and pains that seem to be an increasingly regular part of our lives, and we've been aware, as well, of frequent mental lapses. Furthermore, we're conscious of the loss of many friends and loved ones over the course of years. But confronting our own ever-nearer death is another thing entirely.

And what happened to that other 85 to 90 percent of our life that's behind us? We could recount the highlights of those years in five minutes: graduations, birthdays, weddings, anniversaries, children's births, career moves, travel adventures, and a dozen or so other highs and lows that stick in our memories. Seems like those years flew by in a flash.

The ultimate reality, however, is that one of the five ways of leaving our body has each of our names. Although we cannot exert total control, by reviewing the takeaways scattered throughout each of the preceding chapters, we can proactively try to influence the way we want to pass on. We cannot, of course, control whether or not we will die because dying is inevitable; but we may potentially have some influence over how our death occurs.

Or maybe, on the other hand, is it best to just go on with our lives and not think about such matters? Then, when Death calls our name, we simply answer the call whenever and however it comes!

EPILOGUE

To stave off the possibility that an alert reader challenges my listing of these five ways of dying as not being all inclusive, I add here two more ways that people can die. These two ways also both begin with the letter "A." However, because they are beyond our control, I have not included them in my 5-ways list. Both these possibilities are mentioned in the Christian Bible, the Hebrew Bible, the Upanishads, the Gita, the Tora, and the holy scriptures of other religions.

I refer to **ARMAGEDDON** and the **APOCALYPSE**.

ARMAGEDDON
The Battle of Armageddon, a term that comes from the Book of Revelation in the Christian Bible, is foreseen as a major war that will take place towards

the end of time when the armies of all nations will rise up against each other. The Christian idea is of a final battle between good and evil.

According to Islamic tradition, Jesus' return as a Messenger of Islam will be preceded by wars led by the Mahdi (the rightly-guided one) and by the appearance of the Dajjal (the Antichrist). Armageddon has been also mentioned in some Islamic traditions as the Great Battle that will precede the Day of Judgment. In a general sense, Armageddon is also used to describe any catastrophic or decisive event that threatens the survival of humanity or the planet.

APOCALYPSE

Whereas Armageddon is characterized as the end of the world as a result of warring armies, the Apocalypse portends the end of the world as the result of a natural disaster. Examples include an asteroid collision with the Earth, a global flood, a pandemic, an all-consuming fire that scorches the planet, massive earthquakes that rip the Earth asunder. Or perhaps the end of the world will be the result of an unnatural, man-made disaster: climate change or nuclear annihilation. In the Judeo-Christian tradition the "Four Horsemen of the Apocalypse," who ride on white, red, black, and pale horses, will bring biblical and spiritual lessons to the Earth during the end of times.

The Apocalypse, according to the Hindu view, is not a single event, but rather a cycle of creation and destruction that repeats itself endlessly. Hindu cosmology holds that the world goes through four ages, or yugas, each with different levels of morality and spirituality. The current age is the Kali Yuga, the most corrupt and degenerate one, which will end with the arrival of Kalki, the final incarnation of Vishnu, the preserver god. Kalki will destroy the wicked and restore righteousness, and then the world will dissolve and be reborn again in a new cycle.

As with Hinduism, the Apocalypse in Judaism is not a single event, but a process that involves the end of the current world order and the beginning of a new one. God will redeem the Jewish people, restore the kingdom of David and the Temple in Jerusalem, and bring peace and justice to the world. The Apocalypse in Judaism is also referred to as the "end of days," a phrase that appears several times in the Tanakh, the Hebrew Bible.

According to Buddhist cosmology, the Apocalypse is characterized by moral decay, social unrest, and religious hypocrisy. The Buddhist text, Kalachakra Tantra, describes a future war between the forces of light and darkness that will lead to a purification and the dawn of a golden era.

NONAGENARIAN HANDBOOK

But let's set Apocalypse and Armageddon aside to concentrate on just getting through our Octogenarian years and enjoying a safe, healthy lifestyle. After all, it's only nine more years—or less— until we become Nonagenarians. And what Octogenarian doesn't want to be a Nonagenarian, if they consider the alternative? By then, watch for my next book:

THE NONAGENARIAN HANDBOOK
THE END

ABOUT THE AUTHOR

...and this shirt was given to me on my birthday two years ago.

At age 39, Peter Schroeder had a dream job in Europe managing his own company and was happily settled with his wife and their six-month-old twin sons and two pre-teen daughters. Then terrible back pains sent him back to the States. Doctors diagnosed multiple myeloma, a fatal bone-marrow cancer. Despite surgery, chemo, and radiation therapy, they gave him a prognosis of two years to live.

His disease had been caused by his previous career: working for six years as an engineer with Sandia Laboratories, one of the nation's three nuclear weapons laboratories. He spent three years at the Nuclear Atmospheric Testing Range in the Marshall Islands and an additional three years in underground nuclear testing at the Nevada Test Site, located 65 miles northwest of Las Vegas.

The frequent exposure to nuclear radiation throughout these years later caught up with him and brought on this said-to-be terminal disease.

Given only a short time to live by his Western doctors, he sought out alternative medical systems that led him to Ayurvedic healers in India where he moved with his family for three years. His imminent mortality propelled him to contemplate the multiple aspects of death and served as the stimulus to write this book.

The dire prognosis was wrong. Thanks to the Ayurvedic treatments—and to the amazement of his Western doctors—Schroeder regained his health and returned to Seattle to raise his children.

Now in his mid-eighties, Schroeder and his wife divide their time between homes in Seattle, Washington, where they spend summers cruising on their boat in the San Juan Islands; and Sonoma, California, where they tend to their Syrah vineyard and boutique winery.

Schroeder grew up in Louisville, KY. He earned a Bachelor of Science Degree in Engineering/Physics from Princeton University, a Master of Science Degree in Electrical/Nuclear Engineering from University of New Mexico, and an MBA Degree from Stanford University Graduate School of Business.

www.ingramcontent.com/pod-product-compliance
Lightning Source LLC
Chambersburg PA
CBHW060518090426
42735CB00011B/2284